Gift/ Saudi Arabian Oil Company 2006

Gift/ Saudi Arabian Oil Company 2006

Dedication

Saudi Aramco understands that its enormous business success is due to three factors: natural resources, leadership and our people.

Saudi Arabia was blessed with reserves of both crude oil and natural gas in abundance. For this beneficence, we remain thankful to God.

These natural resources are of no value, however, without vision. In this regard, we thank the nation's leaders, who over the years have guided the company and placed great trust and responsibility in its employees.

Finally, we thank the employees themselves who provided the drive and ingenuity required to find, produce and deliver the Kingdom's oil and gas resources. It is the men and women of Saudi Aramco who rolled up their sleeves and made it all happen.

This book is dedicated to the people of Saudi Aramco – past, present and future.

السعودية ارامكو
Saudi Aramco

The Energy Within
A Photo History of the People of Saudi Aramco

Edited by Kyle L. Pakka

The Saudi Arabian Oil Company (Saudi Aramco)

Dhahran, Saudi Arabia

www.saudiaramco.com

Designed and printed by Afkar Promoseven, Dammam, Saudi Arabia

Acknowledgments

The following people contributed to the creation of *The Energy Within:*

- Design concept by Mounirah A. Mosly
- Khalid A. Afandi • Eyad M. Ajaj • Jamil F. Aldandany • Robert M. Arndt
- Mohammad Aslam • Fahad S. Al-Aziz • Saad S. Azzahri • Jasmine A. Bager
- William E. Bradshaw • Theodore J. Brockish • David R. Cherrington • Arthur P. Clark
- Mona S. Hassan • Ahmed H. Al-Hunjul • Meshal M. Al-Jehani • Thomas H. Keith
- Jamal T. Kheiry • Robert W. Lebling • Nasser A. Al-Nafisee • Gregory C. Noakes
- Alex Padippurathu • Honorio Nor Pangan • Janis E. Patton • Thomas A. Pledge
- Richard J. Snedeker • Shawki M. Al-Sukairi • Muhammad A. Tahlawi
- Joseph X. Thazhath • Rogelio Z. Tuazon • Bradley D. Wilkinson
- The Saudi Aramco Community Heritage Gallery

Contents

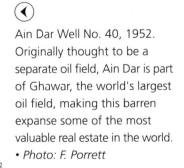

Ain Dar Well No. 40, 1952.
Originally thought to be a
separate oil field, Ain Dar is part
of Ghawar, the world's largest
oil field, making this barren
expanse some of the most
valuable real estate in the world.
• *Photo: F. Porrett*

Preface

The company that we now know as the Saudi Arabian Oil Company, or Saudi Aramco, has its origins in a palace that was once outside of Jiddah, where in 1933, the Saudi government and the Standard Oil Company of California completed a concession agreement that would lead to the discovery of the greatest energy reserves the world has ever seen, thus speeding the rapid transformation of Saudi Arabia into a modern nation-state.

The oil and gas were always in Saudi Arabia — an untapped ocean of energy, waiting for history to catch up. What was needed was an infusion of human energy and vision: the energy within. These qualities were found in the earliest employees, Saudi, American and other nationalities.

They came from villages and towns across Saudi Arabia in the days when it took a week or more of arduous travel to make the journey from Jiddah to the camp at Dhahran, itself just a clutch of simple frame houses and workshops. They came from the Depression-wracked United States, drillers and tool pushers from Oklahoma and Texas, geologists from the Dakotas and California. They crossed the Arabian Sea from India. Later, they came from across the Middle East, from Egypt and Palestine, and from further afield, from Pakistan and the U.K., from South Africa and New Zealand.

The people of Saudi Aramco today are the proud inheritors of a unique history. There are families, Saudi and American, who are in their fourth generation with the company, and employees hail from more than 50 nations.

For the first few years of the concession, geologists, accompanied by their indispensable Saudi guides, ranged across the deserts by car and, later, over them in a Fairchild 71 aircraft, developing an understanding of the structure and stratigraphy of the peninsula. Wells were drilled and a rough exploration camp was built near a cluster of rocky *jabals*, or hills. A strong alliance was formed in those early days, as both cultures toiled to find the natural resource that would lift the Kingdom from economic hardship, and as they strove to accommodate and understand each other's differences.

After five years of hard work, in March 1938, Dammam Well No. 7 came in with commercial quantities of crude oil. The following year, King 'Abd Al-'Aziz Al Sa'ud visited Ras Tanura to witness the first crude oil tanker shipment leaving the Kingdom, a moment that signaled the beginning of Saudi Arabia's prominence as a key supplier of energy to the world.

In the years since then, the company — first known as the California Arabian Standard Oil Company (Casoc), then the Arabian American Oil Company (Aramco) and now Saudi Aramco — has produced more than 100 billion barrels of oil, fueling the growth of the world economy and helping to raise global standards of living.

Along the way, there were symbolic milestones for the company, the Kingdom and the world at large, such as the historic meeting between King 'Abd al-'Aziz and U.S. President Franklin Delano Roosevelt in 1945, which set the tone for the two countries' partnership, one based on mutual interests and respect, and a vision of Saudi Arabia's future importance in the region and in the world.

There have been other meetings and other alliances, as the company grew from an oil producer to a fully integrated, global energy company with partnerships in the Americas, Europe and the Far East.

There were milestones in the company's unique and colorful history, from the first cars and airplane in the Eastern Province, to the fire at Well No. 12 and the Italian air raid of 1940; from the construction of the Trans-Arabian Pipeline and the discoveries of Safaniya and Ghawar, the world's largest offshore and onshore oil fields, to the eradication of malaria and the airing of Aramco television; from the Master Gas System and the building of a supertanker fleet to world-class mega-projects such as Shaybah, Hawiyah, Haradh and Qatif.

One accomplishment stands above all the others: In little more than one generation, the sons of Saudi herdsmen, farmers and fishermen became geologists, engineers and technicians; in turn, their sons have become the managers and executives of an international company of nearly 53,000 employees and the largest supplier of crude oil and natural gas liquids in the world.

The pace of change in the company and in local communities has been breathtaking. Instead of a single barge transporting oil from al-Khobar to Bahrain, thousands of ships call at the company's ports every year, delivering vital petroleum products to nations around the globe.

Where once employees lived in palm-frond *barastis* and simple wood or block homes, more than 52,000 new homes have been built through the company's home ownership program. Where once the sons and daughters of Saudi employees had rough schools or no school at all, the company has built and maintains 139 government-operated schools.

What hasn't changed is the spirit of the people, their determination and will, and their commitment to the company and its pledge to remain the world's most reliable supplier of petroleum energy.

What would the pioneers of the company think if they visited Saudi Aramco today, coming ashore at Jubail on the east coast as the first geologists did? Instead of a small fishing village, they would see a sprawling industrial city; in place of a windswept desert and rocky *jabals*, they would see the modern houses and business towers of Dhahran, and nearby, the gleaming glass-and-steel cities of al-Khobar and Dammam.

When they began drilling in the Dammam Dome, did they dream of the day when maximum sustained oil production capacity would exceed 10 million barrels per day?

Sitting in their tents and their early wooden houses, with limited access to supplies and basic comforts hard to attain, did they envision air-conditioned offices and homes, restaurants, swimming pools and communities landscaped with trees, flowers and grass?

Would they have believed the company that struggled through World War II with a skeleton crew now manages the world's largest known reserves of crude oil, leads the world in crude oil production and exports, is the top exporter of natural gas liquids (NGL), and is one of the world's largest producers of natural gas and refined petroleum products?

Not only did the people of this company have these dreams, their energy and optimism helped make them come true. The images in this book are a testament to that fact.

His Excellency Shaykh 'Abd Allah as-Sulayman, Saudi Finance Minister, and Mr. Lloyd N. Hamilton, lawyer and negotiator for Standard Oil of California (Socal), sign the concession agreement, May 29, 1933, in Khuzam Palace in Jiddah. • *Photo: K.S. Twitchell*

Dhahran through the years

(▲) Dhahran was a wildcat drilling camp on top of the geological formation known as the Dammam Dome in March 1938, when this photo was taken from atop nearby Jabal Dhahran. That month, almost five years after the signing of the concession agreement between the Saudi Arabian government and Standard Oil Company of California, there were 620 Saudis, 56 Americans, and 41 Bahrainis, Indians and others on the payroll. Oil was discovered in commercial quantities this same month, prompting the rapid expansion of the camp and its workforce. By the end of the year, there were 2,745 Saudis, 236 Americans and 104 people of other nationalities at work. Lester Hilyard, who took the photograph above, was a driller on Dammam Well No. 7, the discovery well, later renamed "Prosperity Well." • *Photo: L. Hilyard*

(▲) In 1993, as Saudi Aramco celebrated its 60th anniversary, a pair of company employees with a penchant for history scouted out the spot from which the 1938 panoramic photo of Dhahran had been taken to document the changes wrought in the intervening 55 years. • *Photo: A.G. Waine*

Sometime between 1942 and 1944, a photographer climbed to the top of a drilling rig to take this 180-degree panorama of Dhahran from the west. World War II caused the evacuation of all the American wives and children and about half of the American men. The Ras Tanura refinery was shut down, drilling suspended and new construction stopped. The new fields of Abu Hadriya and Abqaiq were shut in and the tank farm and terminal idled. Still, the skeleton crew, numbering about 1,600 Saudis, 82 Americans and 84 other foreign employees at its lowest point in mid-1942, maintained production of 10,000 to 12,000 barrels of oil per day for shipment by barge to the Bahrain refinery. • *Photo: courtesy Steve Furman collection*

This 1993 Dhahran panorama, taken from the 80-foot ladder of a fire department truck, is the same view as the upper photo. The company numbered 46,000 employees from 50 countries, with Saudis making up about 75 percent of the total. This same year, Saudi Arabia became the world's leading producer of crude oil, passing the United States and the combined total of the states that made up the former Soviet Union. • *Photo: A.Y. Al-Dobais and A.A. Latif*

1930 - 1939: Origins

1930
F.A. Davies, later a company president, while looking for oil in Bahrain, eyes the eastern shore of Saudi Arabia and is convinced the mainland holds promise as well.

1931
Mining engineer Karl S. Twitchell begins a journey across the Arabian Peninsula, looking for water resources, mineral outcrops and oil seeps.

1932
King 'Abd al-'Aziz, encouraged by Twitchell's reports, commissions him to contact oil or mining companies in the United States interested in concessions in Saudi Arabia.

1933
On May 29, the oil concession agreement is signed between Saudi Arabia and Standard Oil Company of California (Socal). On November 8, a subsidiary, California Arabian Standard Oil Company (Casoc), is created to manage the concession.

1934
Aerial reconnaissance begins with the arrival of the company's first airplane, a Fairchild 71.

Dhahran, 1936 • Photo: R. Wells

1935

The first test well is drilled at Dhahran into the Dammam Dome.

Work begins on a pier at al-Khobar.

1936

Texas Co. (now Chevron Corporation) acquires a 50 percent interest in Socal's concession.

1937

A company geologist, Max Steineke, crosses the Arabian Peninsula both ways, gaining a comprehensive idea of the structure and stratigraphy of the peninsula, on which all subsequent geological knowledge is built.

1938

In March, Dammam Well No. 7 at Dhahran strikes oil in commercial quantities.

First crude oil export shipment from the Kingdom is transported by barge to Bahrain.

1939

The first tanker load of Saudi crude oil is shipped from Ras Tanura.

Schuyler B. "Krug" Henry and Robert P. "Bert" Miller, the first two American geologists with Standard Oil Company of California (Socal), arrived in Jubail, Saudi Arabia, September 23, 1933. J.W. "Soak" Hoover, the third American geologist, disembarked in al-Uqayr October 22, with a mechanic, a helper and two drivers. This photo, taken the following day, shows one of three Ford touring cars being unloaded from a dhow, the traditional sailing vessel of the Arabian Gulf, at the al-Uqayr pier near Hofuf. The ports of al-Uqayr and Jubail were principal ports of entry for the fledgling company prior to the development of the pier at al-Khobar in 1935. When this photo was taken, al-Uqayr basically consisted of a caravanserai, customs post and fort.
• *Photo: K.S. Twitchell*

A few days after the arrival of J.W. "Soak" Hoover, the first exploration camp is set up on the Dammam Dome, nine miles (14 km) south of the village of Dammam. Geologists Hoover, Schuyler B. "Krug" Henry and Robert P. "Bert" Miller and a Saudi assistant pose in camp alongside two of the Ford touring cars, October 27, 1933. • *Photo: K.S. Twitchell*

Market day in the old city of Hofuf, seen from the company's branch office, October 12, 1933. Hofuf, the central city of the al-Hasa Oasis, was, at the time of this photo, the capital of the Eastern Province.

At the end of their first month, in late September 1933, Robert P. "Bert" Miller and Schuyler B. "Krug" Henry scouted Hofuf as a possible location for a headquarters. Jubail proved more advantageous for early exploration forays and for bringing in supplies from Bahrain, but the company did maintain a branch office in Hofuf, located in a house rented from the great merchant family of Shaykh Abd ar-Rahman Al-Gosaibi, Bahrain agents of King 'Abd al-'Aziz.
• *Photo: K.S. Twitchell*

Cargo camels, seen here near Jubail during the second field season of 1934-35, supplement cars and trucks and help supply wildcat exploration camps, airplane bases and gasoline dumps.
• *Photo: J. Mountain*

The Fairchild's crew in 1935: left to right, R.C. "Dick" Kerr, Joe Mountain and Russ Gerow. Mountain and Gerow arrived in the fall of 1934, at the start of the second field season. Mountain replaced Charley Rocheville as co-pilot, and Gerow was a mechanic and photographer. • *Photo: M. Steineke*

In this undated photograph, Max Steineke alights from the company's first aircraft, Robert P. "Bert" Miller is in the doorway, and Joe Mountain is at the controls. The original concession agreement included the company's right to use an airplane for exploration work. R.C. "Dick" Kerr was hired in September 1933 to do aerial reconnaissance, and he oversaw the purchase of a plane, a Fairchild 71 from the Kreider-Reisoner plant in Hagerstown, Maryland.

The craft came with a hole in the bottom for taking vertical photographs, a removable window on each side for taking oblique photos, and oversize tires. Charley Rocheville, Kerr's co-pilot and mechanic, designed an extra gas tank, leaving space for only four passengers but increasing the cruising radius to 350 miles (563 km).

While the aircraft was being modified, Kerr spent two weeks in Rochester, New York, home of Eastman Kodak. There, he and Kodak researchers developed special methods for processing photographic film in the harsh desert conditions.

The plane, shipped from New York to Alexandria, Egypt, and then flown via Cairo, Gaza, Rutbah Wells, Baghdad and Basra, arrived in the spring of 1934. The plane was used to map and photograph the region and, toward the end of April, to establish two geologists in a camp 160 miles (257 km) west of Jubail.
• *Photo: J.W. Hoover / Saudi Aramco World / PADIA*

In anticipation of the arrival of the Fairchild airplane from Dhahran in 1935, workers unload aviation fuel, hauled in a pickup truck from the Linah dump site, which was established by camel caravan on the edge of the Dahna Sands near the Iraq border. Geologists began the task of mapping Arabia by flying straight, six-mile (10-km) routes, sketching everything they saw: settlements, oases, hills, *wadis* (dry riverbeds) and caravan routes. Previous maps were based on observations of early explorers and, in al-Hasa, for example, were off by as much as 25 miles (40 km). The Casoc geologists established precise east-west and north-south baselines and worked out a network of aerial triangulation tied in with measurements from the ground. • *Photo: J. Mountain*

An exploration party prepares to leave Dhahran for the Rub' al-Khali, or Empty Quarter, in January 1938. Left to right are Jerry Harriss, a geologist; Shauby and Ibrahim, drivers; Mohammad ibn Abdul Latif, helper; Salih, cook; Saud, Khumayyis ibn Rimthan, and Mohammad ibn Sulayman, soldiers and guides; and Tom Barger, geologist. The departure of exploration parties from Dhahran in the fall and winter, and their return in early summer, was an annual event until air-conditioning enabled year-round work. This party was bound for the Yabrin oasis, 250 miles (402 km) southwest of Selwa, near the border with Qatar, and then further southeast, behind the Trucial Coast of Oman. These early exploration trips often ventured into areas seldom before visited by foreigners.

The geologists brought with them new technology and scientific understanding, but they depended on the inherent knowledge and wisdom of the Saudis, especially that of the guides such as Rimthan whose skills became legendary in the company. Barger would go on to become President and CEO and retired in 1969 as Chairman of the Board. • *Photo: T.C. Barger*

⊙

Max Steineke is widely recognized as the person most responsible for the discovery of oil in Saudi Arabia. A graduate of Stanford University, Steineke was a senior geologist for Socal when he requested an assignment with the Saudi Arabian venture. He arrived in Dhahran in the fall of 1934. In the days before seismic surveying was widely practiced and accepted, geologists such as Steineke relied on mapping, aerial surveys and hands-on field work, as can be seen in this photo from 1935. Steineke also pioneered structural drilling, in which geologists map structures by drilling a grid of shallow wells.

In March and April 1937, he and Floyd Meeker crossed the Arabian peninsula on a field trip that provided insights regarding the structure and stratigraphy of the peninsula, eventually leading to the discoveries of the Abqaiq and Ghawar fields. It was Steineke who backed the decision to drill deeper at Dammam No. 7 when the company was on the verge of halting exploration.

Steineke received the Sidney Powers Memorial Medal Award, the highest honor bestowed by the American Association of Petroleum Geologists, in 1951. • *Photo: unknown*

⊙

The entire contingent of American personnel, except for Joe Mountain, who took the picture, pose for a photograph in Jubail on October 26, 1934. The first headquarters for Socal's operations in Saudi Arabia was Jubail, then a small port on the Arabian Gulf.

Max Steineke, J.W. "Soak" Hoover, A.B "Hugh" Burchfiel, Art Brown, Schuyler B. "Krug" Henry, Allen C. White, T.W. "Bill" Burleigh, Tom Koch, Robert P. "Bert" Miller, Felix W. Dreyfus, Richard C. "Dick" Kerr, Charles Rocheville. • *Photo: J. Mountain*

The exploration camp becomes a drilling camp, and materials such as lumber, cement and equipment are brought over from Bahrain through the pier at al-Khobar by camel, car and tractor. This photo of the Dhahran camp and Well No. 1 was taken from the Fairchild 71 airplane in March 1935. • *Photo: R.C. Kerr*

A Casoc party camps near Abu Jifan en route to Jiddah on a trip to visit King 'Abd al-'Aziz, March 1937. Left to right, Lloyd N. Hamilton, Fred A. Davies, M.W. Thornburg and Floyd W. Meeker. Crossing the Arabian Peninsula was still an arduous undertaking, and the party included two sedans, three pickups, drivers, interpreters and a cook. Geologists Max Steineke and Meeker traveled back to Dhahran on their own, exploring for fossils and encountering rain and hail storms along the way.

Davies arrived in Bahrain on May 14, 1930, with the Bahrain Petroleum Company, or Bapco, the Canadian-registered subsidiary of Socal. He chose the site for the first well in Bahrain and, noticing the cluster of hills across the Gulf in Arabia, concluded that the Eastern Province, then known as al-Hasa, was a likely prospect for oil as well. (Oil was struck in Bahrain in June 1932.) Davies returned to Saudi Arabia as general manager of Casoc in the fall of 1935. He also served as Aramco's second president (1940-1947) and later became CEO, 1952-1959. • *Photo: M. Steineke*

J.W. "Soak" Hoover and Jerry Harriss have breakfast in the spring of 1936, the second full season of field work for Casoc, at a spot known as Ghubaiya, southwest of Dhahran.

Hoover, Harriss and Max Steineke took notice of scattered outcrops in the area that were older than the strata between them and the Dammam Dome. Barometric measurements, taken to calculate elevation, revealed the presence of a subtle anticline, dipping northward — the first indications of an immense structure below.

They didn't know it at the time, but they were having breakfast atop the Abqaiq oil field, discovered four years later.
• *Photo: M. Steineke*

CALIFORNIA ARABIAN STANDARD OIL CO.

PRODUCING DEPARTMENT - GEOLOGICAL DIVISION

STRUCTURAL CONTOUR MAP OF THE

DAMMAM DOME
EASTERN SAUDI ARABIA

BY

S B HENRY AND JW HOOVER

JUNE 1934

Schuyler B. "Krug" Henry and J.W. "Soak" Hoover began mapping the Dammam Dome on October 28, 1933. By June of the following year, they had finished their survey, and the field camp broke up for the summer, with seven geologists moving to Dhour el-Choueir, Lebanon, to write up their notes. This map, excerpted above, is the first one of the Dammam Dome, the most promising structure the geologists had surveyed. Their recommended site for Dammam Well No. 1 is noted on the map.

• *Map courtesy Saudi Aramco Reservoir Characterization*

In anticipation of the need for family housing, the first air-conditioned, two-bedroom California-type portable bungalows were shipped to Saudi Arabia in June 1936. The first American wives, Annette Henry and Nellie Carpenter, arrived in the Eastern Province in the spring of 1937. These houses, photographed in 1937, have undergone numerous renovations and are still in use today. • *Photo: M. Steineke*

The second contingent of American wives, bringing with them the first American children in the Eastern Province, arrive at the al-Khobar pier in September 1937, on the British-India boat from Bombay. Pictured here are Erma Witherspoon, Florence Steineke, Nellie Carpenter, Annette Henry, Patsy Jones and Edna Brown. In the front row are Mitzi Henry, Marian Steineke and Maxine Steineke. Not pictured is the fourth child, Marilyn Witherspoon. • *Photo: M. Steineke*

Tom Koch and a young Saudi companion examine a rarity in the deserts of the Eastern Province: hailstones. Koch and Max Steineke were doing geological survey work west and south of Jubail in November 1934 when the hailstorm struck a *sabkha*, or salt flat, known as Rutgah. That same month, while making an aerial traverse of the as-Su'ayyirah region, the Fairchild broke its tail skid. Koch and Steineke fashioned a temporary skid from automobile springs. • *Photo: M. Steineke*

The pier at al-Khobar, built of *faroush*, the shell-like stones and slabs exposed at low tide, takes shape in the early spring of 1935. The first men and supplies waded ashore at Jubail but, as activity increased, one of the first necessities was a pier closer to operations. The task of building the pier was given to petroleum engineer Floyd Ohliger, below, in flannel shirt. He was assisted by Ahmed al-Somali, on Ohliger's left. Al-Somali was commonly known as "Mussolini" because he spoke fluent Italian. The pier's location was chosen after examining aerial photographs for reefs and channels. In the first large hiring of Saudi nationals, Ohliger hired men to work on the pier's construction. • *Photo: M. Steineke*

The first well at al-Alat, 20 miles (32 km) northwest of Dammam, stands sentinel over a bleak landscape, 1937. Early results from Dammam No. 1 and 2, while not conclusive, were encouraging enough for the San Francisco office to authorize exploration in the promising area of al-Alat, sufficiently close to be supplied from Dhahran. • *Photo: M. Steineke*

The caravan of Karl S. Twitchell is stuck in the sand, a frequent occurrence before automobiles were outfitted with low-pressure balloon tires for desert driving.

In 1931, King 'Abd al-'Aziz, acting upon the results of discussions with his English friend and companion, H. St. John B. Philby, regarding the possibility of mineral resources, extended an invitation to Charles R. Crane, an American, to visit the country. Crane, a wealthy philanthropist who had worked in Yemen, promised to send the King a mining engineer to examine the country's resources. The engineer was Twitchell.

On the lookout for water, minerals and oil seeps, he crossed the peninsula twice in 1931 and 1932, thus becoming the first American engineer to visit the Arabian Gulf coast. Twitchell was put on retainer by Socal to assist in obtaining a concession from the Kingdom.

After the concession agreement was signed, Twitchell became Casoc's representative in the Kingdom and made three more cross-country trips to help establish the company's operations in the Eastern Province. Photographed on the road to al-Hasa on November 5, 1933.
• *Photo: K.S. Twitchell*

The *Calarabia*, one of Casoc's small launches used to ferry personnel and supplies back and forth from Bahrain, leaves the al-Khobar pier in 1936.

On July 5, 1938, the *Calarabia* left al-Khobar on its bi-weekly trip to Bahrain. Halfway there, at 10 a.m., a fire broke out, followed by an explosion. Two Americans lost their lives: Charles and Pauline Herring. The explosion threw Eid ibn Said, two other Saudis — one of whom was badly injured — and Al Carpenter, also in bad shape, into the Gulf. The Saudi crew rigged a raft from floating wreckage, and the four men held onto it as best they could, but the badly injured Saudi died. Before dawn, ibn Said, who joined Casoc on April 8, 1936, as a small crafts captain, and his fellow crewman noticed that Al Carpenter needed aid, and from then until their rescue at noon, they held onto him, saving his life. • *Photo: M. Steineke*

'Ajab Khan, an interpreter originally from Peshawar, now in Pakistan, proves invaluable to the small band of geologists as they struggle to adapt to a new culture. Photographed in 1934, 'Ajab Khan went on to enjoy a long career with the company and after retirement, as a private businessman. • *Photo: J.W. Hoover*

Ras Tanura, a long, low sand spit jutting out into the Gulf and the former site of an Ottoman coaling station, was chosen as the site of Casoc's port. The first tanker of crude oil was loaded May 1, 1939, and on June 26, the tanker *El Segundo* began regular trips every 60 hours from Ras Tanura to the Bapco (Bahrain Petroleum Company) refinery on Bahrain. This photo, taken in 1939, shows the old customs house in the background.
• *Photo: T.L. Lenzen*

Portable housing arrives in Ras Tanura by truck, 1938. With commercial production announced to King 'Abd al-'Aziz on October 16, 1938, extensive plans were drawn up for rapid expansion, including the creation of a major port facility at Ras Tanura with crude oil tanks, submarine loading lines, moorings for deep-draft vessels and a service road and pipeline connecting the facilities to Dhahran, 40 miles (64 km) south. • *Photo: T.L. Lenzen*

Dammam No. 12 burns out of control, its 135-foot (41-m) steel derrick collapsed from the intense heat. For the small contingent of men in Dhahran, unequipped and thousands of miles from supplies, the well fire was a defining moment in the company's life.

The fourth large producing well in the Arab Zone, No. 12 was spudded in on October 23, 1938, and on July 8, 1939, a crew was readying to test-perforate a layer more than 4,600 feet (1,402 m) deep when, for a reason that has never been firmly established, the well exploded. Accounts vary, but two to five employees lost their lives in the fire. For 10 days, every hand pitched in to fight the blaze. Asbestos screens and masks came from Bahrain, and London managed to send asbestos suits and other gear, but it was the ingenuity of the Aramco men who improvised a solution, using a heavy, remote-operated D-clamp to squeeze shut a bypass line to extinguish the fire.
• *Photo: Nestor Sander Collection / Saudi Aramco World / PADIA*

An early, unidentified well blows traces of oil in 1938.

Casoc began drilling for oil in Saudi Arabia on April 30, 1935, when Dammam No. 1 was spudded in. No. 1 went down to below 3,200 feet (975 m) and showed signs of oil and gas but not in commercial quantities. Dammam No. 7, Casoc's first deep test hole, was spudded in on December 7, 1936. A string of accidents, cave-ins, lost drilling bits and a gas blowout at the end of 1937 dampened hopes.

In the spring of 1938, Max Steineke, back at Casoc's office in San Francisco, was asked by executives if their Arabian venture should continue. "Drill deeper," he said.
• *Photo: S.B. Henry*

Les Hilyard and his Saudi drilling crew pose on the steps of No. 7 in 1937-38. A typical drilling crew of the time consisted of an American driller, an assistant driller and 12 Saudis.
• *Photo: L. Hilyard*

To the layman's eye, this telegram, dated March 4, 1938, is a jumble of technical specifications, but to the officers of Casoc back in San Francisco — and to King 'Abd al-'Aziz in Riyadh — this is the news they all had been waiting for five long years: Dammam Well No. 7 had come in, flowing in commercial quantities at 1,585 barrels a day. Three days later, it was flowing at 3,690 barrels a day. Saudi Arabia had become an oil-producing nation. • *Telegram courtesy Saudi Aramco Reservoir Characterization*

MARK **X** TO SHOW KIND OF TELEGRAM, CLASS OF SERVICE AND TELEGRAPH LINE IN PROPER SECTIONS.

Dammam #7

CONFIRMATION	
TRANSLATION	
FOR TYPIST	

TELEGRAM—G. O. 2

SENT VIA

POSTAL	
WESTERN UNION	
FEDERAL	
S. O. CO. OF CAL. LINE	
RADIO	
PAC. TEL. & TEL.	

CLASS OF SERVICE

FAST DAY MESSAGE		DAY LETTER		NIGHT MESSAGE		NIGHT LETTER		CABLEGRAM		RADIOGRAM	

TO.... **E. A. SKINNER** ....

.... **S.F.** ....

CITY **ARABIA**

DATE **MARCH 4, 1938** TIME....

#165 - <u>Well #7</u>   4694' (same) test interval 4620-4694 valve open 58 minutes through 3/4 inch tester and surface bean for 15 minutes flowed 10,900 M.C.F. gas rate and flowed at the rate of 1585 bbls. per day oil API gravity of 33.8° cut 2% bottom sediment and water with pressure of 940 lbs. per square inch well-head and pressure of 120 lbs. per square inch separator in awkward position for shutting in _____? on account of leak Stop Drill pipe rise 360 top 150 oil then 30 black sulphurous muddy water water analysis shows 5170 parts salt per million and 180 mud Stop Coring and testing ahead in stages.

His Majesty King 'Abd al-'Aziz is welcomed aboard the *D.G. Scofield* during his first visit to Casoc's operations in Dhahran and Ras Tanura. On May 1, 1939, King 'Abd al-'Aziz opened the valve that let the first shipment of oil flow into the first tanker to transport Saudi Arabian crude oil. • *Photo: D.M. McLeod*

The tent city of King 'Abd al-'Aziz rises from the desert near Abu Hadriya, where Casoc had a wildcat exploration camp, April 27, 1939. In the spring of 1939, King 'Abd al-'Aziz and a retinue of 2,000 people in 500 cars journeyed from Riyadh to Dhahran on the first royal visit to Casoc's operations. The royal party reached Dhahran the next day. • *Photo: D.M. McLeod*

1940 - 1949: Foundations

1940
The Abqaiq field is discovered.

First school for Saudi employees opens.

1941
A 3,000-bpd refinery opens in Ras Tanura but is closed six months later due to shortages caused by World War II.

1942
Field mapping is suspended due to wartime limitations of manpower and equipment.

1943
Due to the difficulty of obtaining automotive parts, camel transport is used to supply the distant Jauf camp with diesel oil, gasoline, drilling muds and cement.

1944
The company's name is changed to the Arabian American Oil Company (Aramco).

Abqaiq, 1948 • Photo: R.Y. Richie

1945

Thirty-eight tankers load at Ras Tanura terminal, using submarine lines and a two-berth pier.

1946

The first increment of the permanent administration building is completed and occupied in Dhahran.

1947

The new 50,000-bpd refinery at Ras Tanura completes its first full year of operation.

1948

Standard Oil of New Jersey and Socony-Vacuum Oil (both now ExxonMobil) join Socal and Texaco (now Chevron Corporation) as owners of Aramco.

An 80-bed hospital opens in Dhahran.

1949

Crude oil production of 500,000 bpd is achieved early in the year.

The raw community of Ras Tanura takes shape in the summer of 1945. The recreation hall is on the left, and a dormitory can be seen in the background. With the Second World War drawing to its close, Aramco was caught up in a near-frantic expansion as the anticipated postwar slump in demand for petroleum products failed to materialize.

Still facing shortages of materials and skilled labor, and with work on the refinery at Ras Tanura of critical importance, all employees, including about 800 Americans, lived in temporary housing.

The submarine pipeline from al-Khobar to Bahrain was completed early in the year. At 21 miles (34 km), this was the longest submarine pipeline of this type in the world at the time.

During the year, 38 tankers were loaded at Ras Tanura Terminal, at submarine moorings and at the new pier, for a total of 3.5 million barrels for the year. Now, nearly twice that amount of crude oil is loaded every day at the port of Ras Tanura. • *Photo: R.Y. Richie*

The twin crude distillation units at Ras Tanura were less than a year old when this photo was taken in the summer of 1946.

Late in 1943, in anticipation of a prolonged war effort in the Pacific, the U.S. government allocated scarce steel and other supplies for a large project in Ras Tanura to include a refinery, a tank farm, a marine terminal and a submarine pipeline to Bahrain. With manpower and material in short supply — at one point, drilling, refinery and pier construction crews were enlisted to build bunkhouses to house the influx of employees — the Ras Tanura project dominated Aramco's activities for the better part of two years.

The original plan called for two crude distillation units, each with a capacity of 25,000 barrels per day, and associated facilities. The first distillation unit began operations in September 1945 and the second in December. The project was completed on schedule, a remarkable achievement under the circumstances.

By 1949, the refinery, through a series of modifications, had increased its capacity to 127,000 barrels a day. • *Photo: R.Y. Richie*

A diesel locomotive, having been trucked across the desert, is placed on the tracks of the new railroad, 1949. As Aramco underwent rapid post-war expansion, one serious obstacle was the transportation of material from port to site. Cargo ships were offloaded to barges, which were then towed to Ras Tanura or al-Khobar. There were few roads in the Eastern Province, and moving cargo was slow.

In response to a request from the government, Aramco formed a new organization, called the Saudi Government Railroad (SGRR), to finance, construct and operate a railroad to connect Dammam on the Arabian Gulf and the capital city of Riyadh, with stops in Dhahran, Abqaiq and Hofuf.

Construction on the railroad began in 1947. The rail link from Dhahran to Abqaiq opened in 1949, and the line to Riyadh began service with the driving of a golden spike in October 1951, ending the weekly camel caravan between Hofuf and the capital. For passenger service, self-propelled diesel-electric trains, called Budd cars, were used.
• *Photo: R.Y. Richie*

Ras Tanura Terminal employees haul in the *Zane Grey*, a large freighter and the first ship to dock at No. 2 shipping wharf, November 1949. This ship was one of 1,228 oil tankers that called at Ras Tanura that year, an average of 102 a month, and they loaded a total of 16 million tons of petroleum products. The terminal also handled more than 100 cargo ships. As part of the project to build the railroad, a new deepwater port at Dammam was built with a two-berth wharf connected to the mainland by a seven-mile-long (11-km) causeway and trestle. The port opened in 1951. • *Photo: N.D.M.*

Two Saudi drilling rig employees, ready to start the drill bit into a well hole, guide the drilling pipe and bit down through the rotary table on the platform of their rig near Abqaiq, May 1949.

In 1949, 11 oil wells were completed at Abqaiq, nearly half of all wells drilled by the company that year.
• *Photo: T.F. Walters*

An inspector walks a section of the Dhahran-Abqaiq pipeline in the summer of 1946. At the time, there was still no road across the sands to Abqaiq, and transportation of personnel and supplies remained difficult. The harsh terrain was made even harsher by the climate — the thermometer in the sand reads 140 degrees Fahrenheit (60 Celsius). By the next year, there were two 14-inch pipelines running between Abqaiq and Dhahran.
• *Photo: R.Y. Richie*

In a photo symbolic of the changes coming to the desert kingdom, an exploration field crew moves through the desert between Hofuf and Yabrin, southwest of Dhahran, while, in the background, Bedouins cover the same ground by camel. This photo, and the one below of an exploration camp, were taken during the 1939-40 field season by Cecil H. Green, a geophysicist with Geophysical Service Inc. (GSI).

On his first of numerous visits to Saudi Arabia, Green was traveling in the company of George Cunningham, Socal's chief geologist. They visited Abu Hadriya Well No. 1, whose location had been chosen, in part, based on seismographic evidence, a new development in exploration. The ideas promoted by geophysicists, based on early seismic data, were not always welcomed by geologists such as Max Steineke. Greene, Cunningham, Steineke and Ed Skinner, the resident manager for Bapco (Bahrain Petroleum Company), visited Hofuf, Yabrin and the edge of the Rub' al-Khali.

Abu Hadriya struck oil in March 1940, at twice the depth of Dammam No. 7, an early vindication for exploration geophysics. Despite their early professional differences, Greene and Steineke became lifelong friends.
• *Photos: C.H. Greene*

Work on the multi-domed roof of a mosque, contributed by the Saudi government, is nearly complete sometime in late 1944 or early 1945. Drilling on the Dammam Dome continues in the background. • *Photo: unknown*

Italian workers chat outside the hospital in the Italian camp at al-'Aziziyah Beach, near al-Khobar in 1947. In the big expansion year of 1944, the company, still understaffed, obtained permission to hire Italian colonists from Eritrea where they had been lured in the heyday of Mussolini, then stranded when the Italian army withdrew from the country in 1941. In mid-December 1944, the first 88 Italians arrived to prepare a camp for another 1,100.

As Saudi workers grew more skilled through the company's training programs, the number of Italians gradually declined, from 1,200 in January 1950 to 110 by the end of 1957. Many of the fine old stone walls and buildings in Dhahran, such as the South Administration building, Dining Hall, and various homes and buildings on the grounds of the U.S. Consulate, were built by Italian stonemasons.

The company, renamed the Arabian American Oil Company, or Aramco, in January 1944, expanded at an astonishing rate as World War II entered its final stages. In December 1943, there were 2,882 employees. One year later, that number had quadrupled to 9,060.
• *Photo: unknown*

This panorama of Dhahran's Saudi camp, taken in January 1946, shows the completed mosque and the mix of housing styles still in use. The wood and palm-frond *barastis* are being replaced with masonry dormitories.

By the end of the year, 15 28-man dormitories were completed in Dhahran, 17 in Ras Tanura and 13 in Abqaiq, with 15 more under construction.

The company also conducted townsite surveys of al-Khobar and Dammam and laid out street lines and lots and devised a plan for making loans to eligible employees who wished to build their own homes.
• *Photo: MacPherson*

His Majesty King 'Abd al-'Aziz, on his second and last visit to Aramco facilities, receives the company's American wives and their children on the Dhahran tennis court, January 25, 1947. The King made the week-long visit partly to reassure the American personnel and their families that, in the wake of World War II, the Kingdom, and the company, were poised to achieve great things. His Majesty, seated on an arm chair on a carpeted dais, and accompanied by James MacPherson, Aramco's chief resident officer, on his right, greeted each of the 200 wives and 100 children, occasionally seating a delighted young boy or girl on his lap. Later the same day, the King, accompanied by several of his sons, returned from his encampment near the Dhahran airport to attend the final soccer tournament match of the MacPherson Cup at the stadium in the Saudi residential camp.
• *Photo: Evelyn Squires collection*

Fahmi Basrawi, center, with Jabal School students, including, second from right, holding a baseball, Ali I. Al-Naimi, future company President, CEO and later, the Kingdom's Minister of Petroleum and Mineral Resources.

Basrawi also organized baseball and volleyball teams, launched the first Aramco taxi service and later taught English, Arabic and arithmetic on the company television station. • *Photo: Basrawi collection*

Teacher Fahmi Basrawi supervises recitation by a Saudi student at the Jabal School, 1947. The Jabal School, which opened April 8, 1944, to a class of about 70 Saudis between ages 8 and 18, was the fourth company school, but the first one on camp and in a permanent building.

In May 1940, a company school for Saudis — employee and non-employee alike — opened in a home rented from Hajji ibn Jassim in al-Khobar. The school soon outgrew its space and a new classroom, a *barasti*, opened. In response to rising demand, a second school opened and then a third, in January 1941.

The company encouraged promising young Saudi employees from the al-Khobar schools to attend the Jabal school, a converted bunkhouse. The students, mostly office boys, houseboys and waiters, worked half time and went to school half time. About the same time, a similar school opened in Ras Tanura, and before a permanent building could be finished, classes were held in the large wooden crate used to ship the first fire engine from the United States.

Among the students at the Jabal School were future scholars, successful businessmen and company executives. • *Photo: R.Y. Richie*

The second increment of the main administration building in Dhahran is open for business, 1947. The first administration building, encompassing the section to the right of and including the stonework entrance, opened the year before. The company, still struggling with wartime shortages of supplies and skilled laborers, completed the second increment, to the left of the entrance, the following year.

The first section was used for the offices of James MacPherson, vice president and chief resident officer; F.W. Ohligher, vice president; T.V. Stapleton, general manager; and their staffs. The original red bricks were prone to disintegrate in rain and sprinkler water and were covered with courses of concrete bricks.

Two additional wings and a second story were added, and the final building, in its U-shaped form, was completed in 1948.

Company headquarters, first located at 200 Bush Street in San Francisco, in 1948 moved to 505 Park Avenue in New York City. On March 5, 1952, chairman of the board Fred A. Davies arrived in Dhahran, marking the day headquarters moved to Saudi Arabia.

This building, now known as South Administration, today houses offices belonging to Land Affairs, Translation and Correspondence, among others. • *Photo: R.Y. Richie*

Opening night for the play *Mr. Roberts* on the outdoor patio in Dhahran, September 30, 1949. The Dhahran Theater Group originated in 1945 and attracted would-be thespians from across the company: engineers, drillers, pipe layers, refinery workers, secretaries and housewives participated in a wide variety of performances. The group, still active today, builds its own sets, installs lighting, paints scenery and plays its own music.

The production of *Mr. Roberts* featured a cast of 37 and drew more than 3,000 people to six performances. The play was the last performed on the outdoor patio before the theater was completed. • *Photo: D.E. Dickey*

In this photo from May 1949, a Cub Scout troop from Dhahran visits with a Bedouin who relates stories of adventure and desert lore. Scouting got its official start in Dhahran and Ras Tanura in 1946. That same year, the Girl Scouts organized on October 31, the anniversary of the Girl Scouts in the United States. The two communities combined counted nearly 40 children as members. • *Photo: T.F. Walters*

Aramco's growing pains are evident in this aerial view of Dhahran taken September 14, 1949. New houses radiate out from the baseball field and, under construction in the center of the photo, is the theater.

Five years previous to this photo, Aramco had around 2,800 employees. By 1949, the company had grown to more than 20,000 people, almost 10 times as large. The same years witnessed a 25-fold increase in oil production, from 20,000 barrels a day to more than 500,000, making Saudi Arabia the fifth largest oil-producing nation in the world. The year before, for the first time, the United States imported more oil than it exported. • *Photo: R.E. Bright*

Two men stand atop an air raid shelter in Dhahran, 1941. Shelters such as this one were built after Italian planes, in a misdirected air raid on October 19, 1940, dropped two or three dozen small 50-pound fragmentation bombs near Dhahran, puncturing an oil flow line and cutting a water main.

In February 1940, there were 371 American employees, 38 American wives and 16 American children in Dhahran, plus 3,300 Saudis, Bahrainis, Indians and other employees. The air raid in October prompted an evacuation of many employees and of all the women and children. By May 1941, more than half the American men were gone and 40 percent of the Saudi workers were off the payroll.

The war forced Casoc to suspend most operations, including drilling in the Abqaiq area, which was just showing indications of being a huge oil field, and shutting down the 3,000 barrel-a-day "teakettle" refinery at Ras Tanura. • *Photo: unknown*

Sections of 30-foot, 30- and 31-inch diameter pipe are unloaded at the port of Beirut, Lebanon, the western supply port for the Trans-Arabian Pipe Line, or Tapline, April 1949. Aramco built a port and camp at Ras Mish'ab, 162 miles (261 km) north of Dhahran on the Arabian Gulf, to support construction from the eastern end of the pipeline. When it was completed in 1950, Tapline was the longest pipeline ever built, at 1,067 miles (1,729 km), as well as the biggest construction project ever financed and built by private industry.
• *Photo: T.F. Walters*

Work crews on the Trans-Arabian Pipe Line, or Tapline, relieve a giant Kenworth truck of its load of 93-foot sections of pipe near Ras Mish'ab, March 1949. The construction project employed more than 1,500 Americans and nearly 15,000 Saudis and other nationalities.

A pipeline shortcut to the Mediterranean had been considered during World War II but it wasn't until early 1948 that work began on a pipeline from Abqaiq to Qatif Junction and thence to Qaisumah, the actual starting point for Tapline. Work proceeded westward from there with work beginning on the eastern end later. The final weld connecting the two sections was made on September 2, 1950. A few months later, the first tanker was loaded with Saudi crude at the four-berth western terminus of the pipeline a few kilometers south of the ancient city of Sidon, in Lebanon.

Tapline's initial capacity was 320,000 barrels per day. In 1957, capacity was increased to 450,000 barrels per day. • *Photo: T.F. Walters*

Radio operators keep in touch with drilling crews and exploration parties via high-frequency radio and a radio-telephone system in 1948. • *Photo: R.Y. Richie*

The original concession agreement in 1933 between Saudi Arabia and what was to become Aramco called for making royalty and rental payments in gold. The initial payment of $250,000 was made to the Saudi Ministry of Finance in gold.

In the period between 1933 and 1945, Saudi Arabia accepted U.S. currency. Payments in gold resumed when the world market price of gold rose above the U.S. government gold standard price of $35 an ounce. Aramco could not obtain gold at that price and asked the U.S. government for help. In order to make these payments, the U.S. government minted special gold bullion in coin form for Aramco. These coins, in mint condition, are now scarce.
• *Shown near actual size*

Payday: An employee in the Accounting Office readies 2,000 silver Saudi riyal coins, Dhahran, 1947. The office was next door to the district manager's office and across the street from the Jabal School on what was called Main Street, a block of a dozen or so single-story buildings. The silvery tinkle of coins being counted by machine often floated out onto the street from the paymaster's window. On Thursdays, Saudi employees would line up in the street to collect their salary. The company paid Saudi employees and Saudi contractors in silver riyals, and also used the coins for other payments. In 1947, the company paid out more than 26 million silver riyals. • *Photo: unknown*

Several Saudi Arab employees catch a cab in the Saudi residential section of Dhahran in December 1948, a sign of the company's continued progress toward improving living conditions for Saudis, 12,226 of whom were on the payroll that month.

By year's end, the company had constructed 154 one-story masonry apartment buildings, like the ones seen here, to replace the *barastis* — simple structures of wooden pole frames with woven palm leaf ceilings, walls and floors — and tents previously used. The minarets of the camp mosque rise over the rooftops.

The company's effects on the local economy can also be seen by the cabs, owned and operated by private Saudi Arab businessmen.
• *Photo: D.E. Dickey / Saudi Aramco World / PADIA*

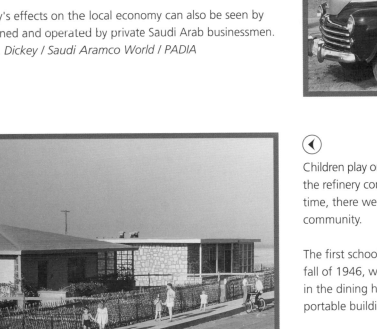

Children play on a quiet street in the residential section of Ras Tanura, the refinery community on the Arabian Gulf coast, fall 1947. At the time, there were about 43 American children living in the young community.

The first school for American children opened in Ras Tanura in the fall of 1946, where 14 students attended class in a makeshift room in the dining hall. The following year, the school moved into a portable building across the street. • *Photo: R.Y. Richie*

Schoolchildren dash for class in the new schoolhouse in Dhahran in the fall of 1947.

The first school for American children opened in October 1945. Classes were held in the living room of a duplex house. By year's end, there were 13 students, and the single teacher, Sam Whipple, taught all the subjects in all eight grades.

School was moved into a different house in the spring of 1946. By the end of the year, a new two-room schoolhouse was open. As the camp's population expanded, the schoolhouse grew too small and the building later became the single men's mess hall and today is the front section of the Dhahran Recreation Library.
• *Photo: R.Y. Richie*

Farm workers stack the wheat harvest from the al-Kharj farms, roughly 50 miles (80 km) southeast of Riyadh, in the late 1940s. Aramco geologists and engineers surveyed the area at the request of King 'Abd al-'Aziz in 1941 to see if underground water resources could be tapped for large-scale farming. The company assumed operation of the farms from the U.S. Agricultural Mission in June 1946. Aramco engineers directed the construction of an 11-mile (18-km) irrigation canal and the installation of water pumps, among other improvements.

Aramco brought in agricultural experts who introduced modern farming techniques. The project initially covered nearly 3,000 acres and produced wheat, alfalfa, maize, melons, vegetables and fruits. An agricultural training school was added later. • *Photo: R.Y. Richie*

An American engineer introduces a Saudi trainee to the slide rule in 1948. The Americans brought something more than new technology with them to Saudi Arabia: They brought the knowledge of how to use that technology. The transfer of this knowledge to a culture without a history of modern industry was accomplished, in part, in thousands of scenes such as this one, in which Americans and Saudis worked side by side.

The Saudi in this photo may never have seen a slide rule, but in little more than a generation, his son and the sons of his countrymen would become geologists, engineers, technicians and managers. • *Photo: R.Y. Richie*

Aramco malaria control personnel examine stagnant water in Dammam for mosquito larvae in 1948. Irrigation canals in the oases of the Eastern Province were later stocked with native *Gambusia* fish, which prey on mosquito larvae.

Following a particularly serious epidemic that swept Dammam and al-Khobar in 1943, company physician Dr. T.C. "Alex" Alexander, who in 1940 became the second American doctor to join the company, undertook a training and education program of his own. As part of the program, Dr. Alexander made weekly trips to al-Khobar and Dammam to see that householders had emptied their water pots to prevent mosquitoes from breeding. • *Photo: F. Ohliger*

1950 - 1959: Momentum

1950
The 1,067-mile (1,729-km) Trans-Arabian Pipe Line (Tapline) is completed from the Eastern Province to Sidon, Lebanon, on the Mediterranean Sea, bringing Saudi crude 3,045 miles (4,900 km) closer to European markets.

1951
Safaniya field, the world's largest offshore oil field, is discovered.

The company completes the 375-mile (603-km) Saudi Government Railroad from Dammam to Riyadh.

1952
Company headquarters is transferred from New York to Dhahran.

1953
To contribute toward the education of the sons of employees through the government school system, the company undertakes the construction of 10 primary schools in the Eastern Province.

1954
Crude oil production exceeds 1 million barrels per day (bpd) in May.

في التأني السلامة وفي العجلة الندامة

1955

First training centers for Saudis are constructed.

1956

The residential community of 'Udhailiyah is built near the heart of the Ghawar field

1957

Aramco TV, the first Arabic-language station in Saudi Arabia and the second in the Middle East, debuts.

Aramco confirms the Ghawar oil field as the world's largest.

1958

Crude oil production exceeds 1 million bpd for a calendar year.

1959

Two Saudi Arabs, 'Abd Allah H. Al-Turayqi and Hafiz Wahbah, join the Board of Directors.

Aramco begins sending promising young Saudi employees to study at U.S. colleges and universities.

There is no high-tech equipment to match the remarkable ability of the desert dwellers known as Bedouins to lead expeditions safely to sites in the deep desert. In the 1930s, Khumayyis ibn Rimthan guided the company's first geologists around the Concession Area, 320,000 square miles (828,796 sq km) of barren, mostly unmapped desert. This photo was taken on an exploration party in 1955 in the Rub' al-Khali, or Empty Quarter. Rimthan, an 'Ajman tribesman from al-Hasa whose skills were so admired that the company named an oil field after him, is on the right. • *Photo: R. Lee*

G.W. "Red" Bird and a Saudi crew map their route to the next exploration camp in the Rub' al-Khali in September 1952. The large Kenworth vehicles are commissary trucks that hauled vital supplies to the work crews deep in the desert every two weeks. Exploration in the forbidding Rub' al-Khali was well under way in the early 1950s, with crews conducting seismic, gravity-magnetic and reconnaissance surveys and structural drilling.

Exploration parties operating in the Rub' al-Khali demonstrated that heavy and light equipment could be used in most of the sand-covered areas and that sufficient water could be developed to support operations in the future. • *Photo: T.F. Walters*

In some areas of the Rub' al-Khali, trailer camps are impractical, and small tent camps, like this one in 1955, are used to house exploration parties. Venturing deep into the desert was and still is risky work: Looming over the tents is a *shamal*, or northerly sand storm, which can dramatically reduce visibility in minutes and last for days.

A surveyor adds to the map of the Rub' al-Khali, overlaying coordinates and gridlines on the shifting dunes.

In previous years, exploration crews would return to Dhahran each June, bringing their equipment in for overhaul and repair. In 1955, one structure-drill party left all its equipment, save for vehicles, on site. Repair crews were flown in to perform overhaul work, saving a round trip of 810 miles (1,300 km) for the heavy equipment. • *Photos: R. Lee*

⊙

Saudi recruits get their first look at the working parts of a drilling rig. This derrick in Dhahran was reserved for training rigmen, assistant drillers and diesel mechanics. During a 14-week course, the trainees drilled a 200-foot hole and went through the other steps needed to create an oil well. Soon they would be in the field helping to fuel the extraordinary 100 percent increase in oil production between 1949 and 1954. • *Photo: T.F. Walters*

⊙

The energy and enthusiasm many young Saudis brought to their jobs are clearly evident in the smile of 'Abd Allah ibn Yousuf al-Husaini, an office boy in Public Relations in Dhahran, 1950. Aramco was a springboard for countless young Saudis eager to develop themselves, their country and the Gulf region.

Al-Husaini joined Aramco in 1948 and worked his way up the company's educational and career ladder, attending the American University of Beirut and Syracuse University in the United States. Initially assigned to Recruiting, he later moved to the Medical Department and then Public Relations where he held various positions, including editor of the weekly English and Arabic newspapers.

Al-Husaini left Aramco in 1972 and relocated to Qatar, where he founded a publishing house and also joined the Foreign Service, serving as consul general of Qatar in India for four years. • *Photo: D.E. Dickey*

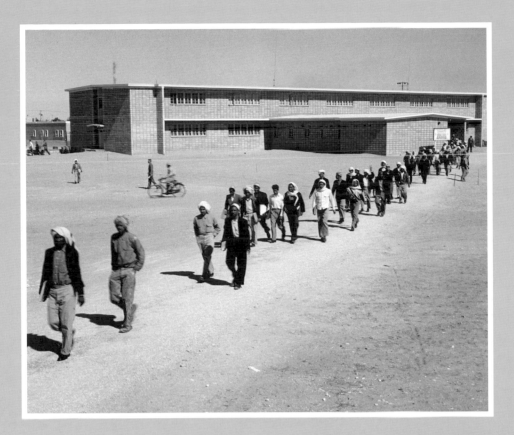

Saudi trainees file out of the new Abqaiq Industrial Training Center (ITC), 1956. This center, and ones like it in Dhahran and Ras Tanura, were the first buildings specifically designed as training centers. They contained between 20 and 24 classrooms plus a science laboratory, a drafting room and a business machines classroom. The three ITCs were built between 1955 and 1957 for a total of $1.1 million.
• *Photo: E.E. Seal*

Today's ships of the desert, Kenworth trucks serve as a lifeline for Saudi Aramco employees wherever they are in the Kingdom. These huge, red trucks have been hauling supplies and equipment across the desert for more than 50 years.

'Abd Allah ibn Husain, at the cab of a Kenworth model 853 in 1955, was the first Saudi to drive a Kenworth truck over sand between Dhahran and Riyadh. The 853 — known as a "deep desert" truck — had a 400 horsepower, V-12 engine and a gross weight of 25 tons. Even larger Kenworth models were used to move rigs and other heavy equipment.
• *Photo: K. Rissas*

(▶)

Aramco announced two spectacular finds in the 1950s: Ghawar, the world's largest onshore oil field, and Safaniya (right), the world's largest offshore field.

The first indications of Ghawar were noted in 1940, when geologists Ernie Berg and Tom Barger were mapping an area on the edge of the Rub' al-Khali desert 200 miles (320 km) southwest of Dhahran. Berg noticed that a dry riverbed, or *wadi*, took a sudden turn for no apparent reason. His detailed mapping revealed the *wadi* was diverted by a dome, the first sign of a huge structural uplift.

In 1948, the company began drilling in the area, striking oil at a place called Haradh. More detailed mapping ensued and this, combined with an oil strike at 'Ain Dar, more than 155 miles (250 km) to the north, pointed to the existence of an enormous geological structure. In 1957, Aramco was able to confirm Ghawar as a single field about 174 miles (280 km) long and up to 16 miles (26 km) wide.

Safaniya No. 1 was drilled in August 1951 on a narrow point of land stretching into the Arabian Gulf, 165 miles (266 km) north of Dhahran. The fully-developed field stretches 31 miles (50 km) across the Gulf in a northeast direction and is about 10 miles (22 km) wide at its widest point. Production began in 1957. • *Photo: B.H. Moody*

(▶)

Suliman Olayan discusses his new LPG truck with Bill McMullen of Aramco, October 20, 1953. This was the first 6,000-gallon tank truck in the Kingdom, supplying customers in al-Hasa with gas for cooking, A/C and heating. Olayan, a pioneer employee of Aramco, later became one of the world's wealthiest men. Initially employed by Aramco as an interpreter in July 1937, Olayan worked a variety of jobs in shipping and receiving. He left the company in 1947, partly at the urging of Aramco, which encouraged promising employees such as Olayan to start their own businesses, thereby expanding the local economy. Olayan started his own trucking enterprise and soon struck an early deal with American construction giant Bechtel Corporation as a contractor on the Tapline project.

Olayan was the founder and chairman of The Olayan Group, which grew into a conglomerate of 50 companies around the world. He is credited with playing a key role in developing the first insurance, electrical-power and gas companies in Saudi Arabia. Suliman Olayan, and many others like him, spread the benefits of Aramco training and support far beyond the borders of the Eastern Province and of the Kingdom itself, playing significant roles in the economic and social development of the Kingdom, the region and the greater world.
• *Photo: O. Oxley*

◀

Muhammad al-Najim assists student typists in a class at Dhahran's advanced clerical training center in Dhahran, 1952. Training of Saudi employees grew phenomenally in the 1950s with the advent of the Aramco Production Training Program, the first organized, company-wide effort to qualify large numbers of Saudis for jobs then being performed by expatriates.

In 1953, 60 percent of all Saudi workers, some 8,200 people, were enrolled in training programs. By the following year, the number of Saudis in higher grade codes was 14 times greater than in 1949.

The challenge and scope of training the Saudi workforce by Aramco personnel, who came from a different culture and who were not native speakers of Arabic, remains unmatched in the history of human resource development in an industrial setting. • *Photo: O. Oxley*

◀

Today, the Eastern Province of Saudi Arabia is malaria free. But for centuries, the disabling and sometimes deadly disease was endemic in the area. In the 1940s, it was estimated that 98 percent of children under age 1 were infected and that 25 percent of adults suffered disabling bouts of malaria each year. Periodic epidemics forced families to abandon homes in oases.

Aramco medical professionals — in cooperation with the government — launched a vigorous anti-malaria campaign in the early 1940s. They toured the province, warning people that malaria was caused by mosquitoes that breed in stagnant water. Villagers were urged to empty their water jars every 10 days to kill the mosquito larvae. The campaign had limited success until powerful new insecticides became available after World War II.

Thanks to a house-by-house spraying campaign, the number of malaria cases in the province plunged by 60 percent between 1947 and 1949. The number of cases on Aramco compounds fell from 2,000 to 94 in the same time span.

Aramco contractors in this 1952 photo are marking a house in Qatif to show it had been sprayed. Spraying continued until 1958, when malaria was finally eradicated from the Eastern Province.
• *Photo: O. Oxley*

The *Flying Camel* arrives on her maiden voyage from New York to Dhahran, August 4, 1952. The aircraft, a DC-6B, replaced the original *Flying Camel*, a DC-4 Skymaster that inaugurated Aramco's transatlantic service in April 1947.

Until widespread commercial jet service finally eliminated the need for Aramco's own transatlantic flights — which ended on January 1, 1961 — the *Camel* and her younger sisters, the *Gazelle* and the *Oryx* (a DC-4), logged more than 17 million miles with 87,600 international passengers and 7.3 million pounds of cargo, made 2,400 Atlantic crossings and completed nearly 14 years of scheduled international service without a single fatality or injury.

The 7,005 air miles between Dhahran and New York were covered in something less than 30 hours flying time. Flight plans varied over the years, but a common schedule was for regular flights to depart from Dhahran for New York every Sunday and Tuesday, arriving on Tuesdays and Thursdays. The New York-Dhahran route departed Wednesday and Friday afternoons. Passengers overnighted in Europe — eastbound at Amsterdam and westbound at Rome.
• *Photo: T.F. Walters*

On September 17, 1957, Aramco introduced television to Saudi Arabia. Aramco station HZ-22, Channel 2, was the first Arabic-language station in Saudi Arabia and the second in the entire Middle East. (An Arabic station was on the air in Baghdad, and a small English-language station operated out of the Dhahran air base.)

Air time was divided about equally between recreational and educational programs. The lineup included science, mathematics and English language classes for local schools as well as adult listeners. Fahmi Basrawi, the former Jabal School teacher, was the first performer on opening night, and he went on to host educational programs on Aramco television for 17 years and also became the celebrated host of a quiz show televised nationally by a Dammam station.

In this photo, Basrawi and Dr. Taibah, a company doctor, host a segment of a weekly program on health education, December 1957. • *Photo: E.E. Seal*

Americans brought their games with them to Saudi Arabia. They organized leagues and held tournaments in sports such as baseball, basketball, bowling, tennis, golf and even polo. Saudis were largely indifferent to those sports but took to soccer as if born to play the game. Soccer developed from informal pickup games played with a rag ball into a popular spectator sport with teams representing Aramco communities. This match between Dhahran and Ras Tanura was played at the Dhahran sports center in 1959. • *Photo: V.K. Antony*

Al-Khobar and Aramco grew up together. By 1954, when this photo of King Sa'ud Street was taken, al-Khobar had grown from a fishing and pearling village of less than a dozen homes to a busy town stretching nearly a mile along the waterfront and about 10 blocks inland. Four years later, a census placed al-Khobar's population at 33,000. The town boasted department stores, groceries, auto repair shops, medical offices, a bank, several restaurants and a soft-drink bottling plant. • *Photo: O. Oxley*

The busiest corner in Dhahran in 1952. These portable buildings housed the community post office, laundry and canteen. In 1985, the Al-Mujamma' Building, containing a post office, bank, barber shop and other services for employees, replaced the portables. The main administration building, now part of a larger complex and known as the South Administration Building, is in the background. • *Photo: T.F. Walters*

◀

Shoppers in the Dhahran commissary in the 1950s enjoy a selection of food and household items nearly unimaginable to the workers who first arrived in the region two decades previously. No longer wildcat camps, Dhahran, Abqaiq and Ras Tanura had grown into true communities with paved streets and sidewalks, libraries, golf courses and tennis courts, bowling alleys, horse riding stables and swimming pools. The desert was made to bloom, and the harsh landscape was softened by grass lawns, trees and flowers. • *Photo: unknown*

◀

A bewildering number of tribal dialects are spoken in Saudi Arabia. Early on, the company recognized this communication problem. Moreover, there were no words in Arabic for the paraphernalia of an oil company. Saudi work teams created their own on-the-job language by imitating the English words for tools and work processes.

The company hired linguists such as Charles Matthews, left, to study the various dialects and develop English language courses for Saudi employees. Here, in 1958, Matthews interviews employees Salim ibn Sa'id al-Bathari, 'Ali ibn Musallam al-Qarawi and Mubarak ibn Sanqur al-Harsusi from the as-Saddwai region in northeastern Saudi Arabia.

The linguists also created a course called Arabic Work Vocabulary for Americans and offered a $50 bonus to any expatriate employees who successfully completed the course. There were few takers. • *Photo: E.E. Seal*

Launched in November 1949, *Aramco World* began as an interoffice newsletter intended to link the company's U.S. offices with "the field." As the company grew, *Aramco World* became a bimonthly educational magazine styled along the lines of such popular U.S. magazines as *Life* and *The Saturday Evening Post*. Historical, geographical and cultural articles helped the American employees and their families appreciate an unfamiliar land and culture.

This cover, from the July 1953 issue, illuminates both the cooperative spirit that Saudis and Americans brought to the early years of the Aramco venture and the cultural differences they faced.

Since the mid-1960s, the magazine has been aimed at a worldwide readership, its articles spanning the Arab and Muslim worlds, past and present, with special attention to their interconnections with the cultures of the West.

Now called *Saudi Aramco World*, the magazine is still distributed six times a year, upon request and without charge, to some 150,000 subscribers in 130 countries and is also available online at *www.saudiaramcoworld.com*.

Two cultures, one world. Susan Kelly, an American, and Faridah Sowayigh, pose in 1952 for a photo to accompany an article in *Aramco World* about the relationship between Saudis and expatriates at Aramco. Faridah was one of the first Saudis to attend the Aramco schools, which had been exclusively for the children of expatriate employees. Both girls were in the sixth grade in Dhahran when this photo was taken. Susan points to her home state of Wyoming, while Faridah marks Saudi Arabia, 7,000 miles apart.
• *Photo: T.F. Walters*

Children living in the Tapline community of Qaisumah head toward the community center in April 1955. The pump house and oil storage tanks can be seen in the background. The Tapline communities, while isolated, were tightly knit. The aerial photo below conveys a sense of the isolation of the Tapline camps.

Completed in 1950, the Trans-Arabian Pipe Line, or Tapline, crossed 1,067 miles (1,729 km) of desert to link the oilfields of Saudi Arabia's Eastern Province with the Mediterranean. It remained fully in use until the early 1970s, when military confrontations in the region crippled the part of the pipeline from Jordan to Lebanon. Delivering oil through Tapline to the Zarga' refinery in Jordan continued until the outbreak of the Gulf War in 1990. Moreover, the development of ultra-large tankers made ocean shipment of oil a more economical alternative.

Towns grew up around the four main pump stations in Saudi Arabia, and the road that paralleled the pipeline became an important Middle Eastern transportation artery. The main Tapline pump stations in Saudi Arabia were located at Qaisumah, Rafha, Badanah and Turaif. Aramco graded sand ramps over pipelines and drilled water wells to ease the impact of the pipeline on the local Bedouin.

It took almost 4.9 million barrels of oil to fill Tapline, and the pump stations and tanks also needed a stock of oil for the line to function. All in all, nearly 6 million barrels of oil were required to keep the operation moving. • *Photos: O. Oxley*

New, bright red 1952 Dodge 4-door sedans for use by Aramco's U-Drive customers are on display in the parking lot in front of the Dhahran Administration Building. The air-conditioned, 140-horsepower V-8s were painted "Aramco" red with large numbers in white that could be easily spotted from a rescue plane if the driver was lost or stuck in the desert. In 1952, when this photo was taken, the company had a fleet of more than 3,200 motor vehicles of all types. • *Photo: T.F. Walters*

'Abd Allah H. Al-Turayqi and Hafiz Wahbah became the first two Saudis to join the Board of Directors when they were elected on May 20, 1959. This formal portrait, with President Norman Hardy at the head of the table, was taken in October 1959. Turayqi, a geologist with a master's degree from the University of Texas, was the Director General of Petroleum and Mineral Affairs for Saudi Arabia. Wahbah was an elder statesman, Saudi ambassador-at-large to the Arab world, former representative of Saudi Arabia in Britain, and a delegate to the 1945 United Nations Conference in San Francisco. • *Photo: E.E. Seal*

This is the first all-Saudi crew to operate a gas-oil separation plant (GOSP) at Aramco. In January 1950, John Hoss, an Abqaiq area power plant operator, began an intensive training program for GOSP operators. By May of that year, a Saudi crew under supervisor Khalil ibn Issa (front of line) took over operations at GOSP-3, a new 100,000-barrel-per-day plant at Ain Dar. Within a year, three more Abqaiq-area GOSPs were being operated by all-Saudi crews. • *Photo: T.F. Walters*

A Saudi mechanic opens the main valve of a well in the Dammam Field, March 1951.

The Dammam Field, the first discovered, produced more than 29 million barrels of oil in 1951 from 30 producing wells. Crude oil production and refinery output for 1951 exceeded the figures from any preceding year.
• *Photo: T.F. Walters*

▲

HRH Crown Prince Sa'ud ibn 'Abd al-'Aziz Al Sa'ud visits a Saudi trade school in Dhahran, January or February 1950. The eldest son of King 'Abd al-'Aziz, Sa'ud succeeded his father upon his death in 1953. The Crown Prince arrived in Dhahran January 23 and spent nearly a month touring company facilities and other sites. On the last day of his visit, February 17, the Crown Prince and 7,000 spectators attended a soccer match between the district all-star teams.

In 1950, the company agreed to a new financial arrangement that gave the Saudi government a 50-50 share in the company's net operating income. Two years later, the 1950 agreement was modified to give the government a 50-50 share in the company's gross income. • *Photo: T.F. Walters*

▲

The first company-built government school stands ready to receive students, Dammam, November 2, 1954. • *Photo: K. Rissas*

▶

Runners are poised to race on the new track as part of the inauguration ceremonies to mark the first company-built government school, December 7, 1954. The local school system, which lacked any taxing authority, had been overwhelmed by the influx of Aramco employees and their families. In

negotiations with the government, Aramco agreed to finance construction of schools and pay for their operation, while the government supplied the curriculum and teachers. The company has constructed more than 135 schools in the Eastern Province since this facility opened in Dammam. • *Photo: K. Rissas*

Aramco schools were the first schools, in the modern sense of the word, in the Eastern Province. In the 1940s, these schools were opened free-of-charge to anyone of any age, employee or not. English was the most popular subject. English was the language of the oil company, and any Saudi who knew a few words of English had a good chance of getting a job. Here, two students of the company's Jabal School in 1950 are being tutored by an older Saudi. • *Photo: unknown*

For hundreds of Saudi employees, the adventure in higher education began at the American University of Beirut (AUB). These employees, strolling the campus in 1953, were among the first to attend AUB on a company scholarship.

At that time, high-potential Saudi employees were sent to AUB for one year to earn a high school diploma. Most of them stayed on to complete two years of college work before returning to Aramco. A few others were allowed to complete the full four-year degree program; it all depended on the needs and inclinations of their sponsoring organization. Aramco also sent Saudi employees to AUB in the summer for specialized, short-term training programs.

These students are, left to right, Mohammed Salamah, Ibrahim Muhtasib, Sulaiman Rubaya, Fahmi Basrawi, Ihsan Tawfick and Abdul Gader Bubshate. • *Photo: unknown*

1960 - 1969: Development

1960

Scholarships for Arab students of nursing are established at the American University of Beirut.

The Organization of Petroleum Exporting Countries (OPEC) is formed.

1961

The first shipment of liquefied petroleum gas (LPG) is loaded onto a tanker at Ras Tanura.

1962

Cumulative crude oil production reaches 5 billion barrels.

1963

The Abu Sa'fah offshore field is discovered.

The College of Petroleum and Minerals (later renamed the King Fahd University of Petroleum and Minerals) is established.

1964

The Berri oil field is discovered.

The first Aramco-built government school for Saudi girls opens.

Offshore drilling platform • Photo: S.M. Amin

1965

The Zuluf offshore field is discovered.

Crude oil production for the year exceeds 2 million barrels per day (bpd).

1966

A two-berth Sea Island loading terminal, built for the largest tankers afloat, begins operation off Ras Tanura.

1967

The offshore Marjan, Karan and Jana oil fields are discovered.

Liftings of crude oil and petroleum products from company terminals exceeds 2 million bpd.

1968

Shaybah field is discovered in the northeastern Rub' al-Khali.

The company becomes the first to produce 1 billion barrels of oil in less than a year.

The Organization of Arab Petroleum Exporting Countries (OAPEC) is founded.

1969

Aramco's first offshore gas-oil separation plant (GOSP) goes on-stream 25 miles (40 km) from Safaniya in the Arabian Gulf.

The third two-berth loading terminal opens at Ras Tanura Sea Island

Aramco's new mobile drilling platform arrives in Suez, August 17, 1966. The rig was fabricated in Vicksburg, Mississippi, in the U.S. and towed to Ras Tanura. After the leg sections were welded in place, the rig was moved in December 1966 to its first assignment in the Berri field. This same year, production from the offshore Abu Sa'fah field was inaugurated.

• Photo: H. Al-Ramli

An Aramco exploration party sets off a large seismic charge near Qaisumah, the location of a Tapline pump station and company community, in January 1963. Five exploration parties were searching for hydrocarbons this year, from the gravel plains in the north to the Rub' al-Khali in the south.

This same year, work was completed on the geographical-geological mapping program established in 1954 by Aramco and the United States Geological Survey under the joint sponsorship of Saudi Arabia and the United States. Revised Arabic and English editions of the 1:2 million geographic map and a new geologic map of the Arabian peninsula were published, making Saudi Arabia one of the most thoroughly mapped areas in the world. • *Photo: B.H. Moody*

C.A. Trogden and Adil Mohammad discuss the day's work at the Berri No. 1 wildcat well campsite in February 1964. Two months later, No. 1 came in as a discovery well. The Berri field, 40 miles (64 km) northwest of Ras Tanura, proved to lie both onshore and offshore. • *Photo: B.H. Moody*

▲

Helicopters enable crews in the Rub' al-Khali to complete about 20,000 feet (6,096 m) of seismic coverage daily, more than double the rate possible in this region without helicopter support. In 1966, Aramco leased for the first time five Bell helicopters to carry men, materials and seismic equipment to areas of the Rub' al-Khali.
• *Photo: B.H. Moody*

▲

The vast sand dunes of the eastern Rub' al-Khali surround Seismic Camp 3 in May 1966. The establishment of this camp marked the beginning of two years of seismic exploration of the subsurface geology of what was at once the most inaccessible, most inhospitable, most rugged — and perhaps most spectacularly beautiful — area yet penetrated by Aramco's exploration teams.

The arid mountains of sand tower above salt-mud flats that barely cover reservoirs of ground water seven times as salty as the sea. In the spring, desiccating winds can raise temperatures well above 110 degrees Fahrenheit (43 degrees Celsius) during 10 hours of the day.
• *Photo: A.L. Yousif*

Seismic Camp 3 is home to around 106 men who stay in the field for up to four weeks at a stretch, October 1967. Crews are rotated back to Dhahran on an Aramco Fokker F-27 that makes one round trip per week carrying personnel and priority cargo. The F-27 and other aircraft attached to the camp land on an airstrip constructed by rolling and packing the salt-mud flats of the *sabkha* with truck tires. Five contract helicopters with motors specially adapted to work in the hot air of the Rub' al-Khali are also stationed at the camp.

The next year, the Shaybah field was discovered in the Rub' al-Khali. • *Photo: T. Eigeland*

Exploration parties in the Rub' al-Khali in June 1967 traverse the dunes aboard Aramco's first fleet of 12 sand buggies, which are used to transport men and equipment for seismic operations. The buggy's large, low pressure tires give the vehicles high mobility in the desert. The buggies later saw service along the Gulf coast, performing seismic work in the inter-tidal zones. • *Photo: B.H. Moody*

The water tower of the College of Petroleum and Minerals, now King Fahd University of Petroleum and Minerals (KFUPM), rises above the desert near Dhahran, 1968. The water tower was one of the first campus projects and, especially when illuminated at night, remains one of the most prominent landmarks in Dhahran.

The Saudi Government established the College of Petroleum and Minerals by royal decree in September 1963, the first facility in the Kingdom devoted to training and research in the petroleum industry. The first Saudi company employees enrolled at the college in 1969 and, that same year, students from the college undertook one-year work assignments with Aramco before returning to the college to finish their degrees. • *Photo: D. Miller*

A 75-ton spheroid from a gas-oil separation plant (GOSP) in Abqaiq was moved to a GOSP at Ras Tanura via a desert route to avoid shutting down power lines and snarling traffic on main roads in 1969. Aramco produced nearly 3 million barrels of oil per day this year, almost a 6 percent increase from the previous year. • *Photo: S.M. Amin*

▲

HRH Crown Prince Faisal ibn 'Abd al-'Aziz Al Sa'ud tours Safaniya, March 1963. During his week-long visit in the Eastern Province, the Crown Prince toured Abqaiq and other company facilities, and attended an open-air rally near the Dammam Railway Station, at which several thousand local citizens were present. • *Photo: A. Mentakh*

▲

Aramco's 6 billionth barrel of crude oil is produced at 11 a.m. on February 19, 1964. In the Aramco oil dispatching center at Abqaiq, oil and gas dispatcher Abdulla M. Al-Sabti receives production rates by radio and telephone. Discussing a dispatching problem are Donald R. Fate, Abqaiq assistant district manager; Subhi M. Sanuri, foreman, Oil Dispatching; Mohammed Al-Dhufair and Safar Yahya, foremen, Producing.

This latest billion-barrel mark was reached 12 years after the company's first billion barrel production milestone on January 4, 1952. In 2004 alone, Saudi Aramco produced more than 3 billion barrels in a single year. • *Photo: V.K. Antony*

▶

The snowcapped mountains of Lebanon form a picturesque backdrop to the Sidon Terminal of Tapline (Trans-Arabian Pipe Line Company) and a company DC-3. Sidon was the end point of the 1,067-mile (1,729-km) crude oil pipeline originating in the Eastern Province of Saudi Arabia.

In December 1960, when this photo was taken, Tapline marked its 10th anniversary. In the course of that decade, the Sidon Terminal loaded 8,191 tankers with 1.2 billion barrels of oil. Tapline was a major outlet for Aramco's westbound crude exports until the early 1970s. • *Photo: unknown*

▶

The Qatif-Abqaiq pipeline No. 5, a 31-mile (50-km), 40/42-inch line, was Aramco's major pipeline project in 1969. One hundred and thirty-five miles (217 km) of pipeline were built during the year, and at year-end, the Aramco pipeline system, excluding flow lines, totalled 2,014 miles (3,241 km).

That same year, Aramco's first offshore gas-oil separation plant (GOSP) went on-stream 25 miles (40 km) from Safaniya in the Arabian Gulf. The GOSP, designed to more efficiently produce present and future oil wells in the Safaniya field, went into operation at an initial rate of approximately 200,000 barrels daily. • *Photo: B.H. Moody*

▶▶

These men are among the hundreds of company maintenance workers taking part in the Test and Inspection of Ras Tanura Refinery in May 1969. For the first time since 1962, the entire refinery was shut down for inspection and repair work. About 500 employees working two shifts completed the task in four days.

The refinery processed 161 million barrels of crude oil, naphtha, natural gasoline and raw liquefied petroleum gas that year, averaging more than 440,000 barrels a day. Up to five grades of eight different products were manufactured at the refinery, with 94 percent of the products exported. • *Photo: S.M. Amin*

Sami A. Labban, left, of Aramco's Agricultural Assistance Development Division, discusses the poultry business with a Saihat farmer in July 1965. Poultry men in the Eastern Province, with assistance from Aramco, moved 1 million dozen eggs to market, double the production of the previous year and a twenty-fold increase over 1960. Vegetable production increased from 2.5 million to 3.7 million pounds, and the gross income of farmers from poultry and vegetables rose above $1 million.

Aramco also installed main irrigation canals, established a nursery and planted soil-stabilizing crops on a 100-acre experimental area as part of the government's Haradh Agricultural Project.

Through loans, the company also contributed to the infrastructures of al-Khobar and Dammam where sewer and water installations capable of serving 50,000 people were nearly complete. • *Photo: B.H. Moody*

Elementary school pupils prepare for exams in the courtyard of their Aramco-built government school in al-Khobar in 1969. Seven new schools were completed or under construction in the Eastern Province that year under an agreement with the government. Five were intermediate schools — three for girls and two for boys — and two were elementary schools for girls. In addition to the seven new schools, the company also constructed seven new wings for existing girls' schools. With the completion of these facilities, Aramco had built a total of 37 schools for the government — 24 for boys and 13 for girls. • *Photo: A.L. Yousif*

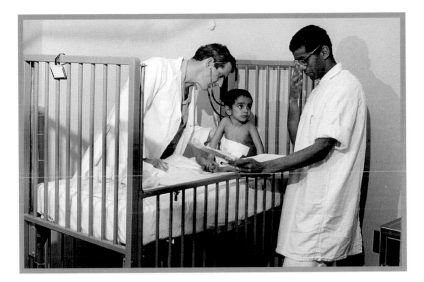

⊙

Dr Warren Devere and Hamid, a Saudi nurse, examine a young patient at the pediatric ward in Dhahran in February 1960. Aramco Health Centers in Abqaiq, Dhahran and Ras Tanura had 409,433 clinic visits from patients during 1960. That same year, immunization programs were established for smallpox, typhoid, paratyphoid, tetanus, diphtheria and, for children, whooping cough and poliomyelitis. The company also established scholarships for Arab students of nursing at the American University in Beirut.
• *Photo: V.K. Antony*

⊙

Medical professionals search for a vaccine against the eye disease trachoma in 1967, the 13th year of joint research between Aramco and Harvard University. By year-end, 145 trachoma virus strains had been typed in preparation for future vaccine trials.

Aramco made an initial grant of $500,000 to Harvard in 1955 for a five-year research program. In 1960, the company made a further grant of $585,000 for an additional five-year period. In 1958, the strains of the trachoma virus found in Saudi Arabia were isolated. While a vaccine was never discovered, the program yielded significant data on the epidemiology of the disease in Saudi Arabia. As the country developed and sanitation improved, the disease became far less prevalent. The project ended in 1974. • *Photo: B.H. Moody*

⊙

Atif Bokhary, left, of the Ministry of Agriculture, Faysal Ruwayha of Agricultural Assistance and Aramco consultant Martin Fogel conduct a survey of free-flowing wells in the Qatif oasis as part of a detailed irrigation study, March 1963. Aramco provided technical assistance to the Saudi government and the Food and Agricultural Organization (FAO) of the United Nations in implementing an experimental farm and training center in Qatif.

In other examples of Aramco's service to local communities that year, guaranteed loans were made to help establish an offset printing shop and a clothing factory in Dammam, and, in the Hofuf area, a million trees were planted by the government under a long-range sand control program developed and recommended by the company.
• *Photo by A. Khan*

(▶) An employee at the Marine Terminal bolts a crude oil loading arm to a tanker berthed at the Ras Tanura Sea Island Terminal, 1967. This same year, two more deep-water berths opened at the Terminal with a fifth near completion. The 2,694 tankers loaded at Ras Tanura took on 753 million barrels of crude oil and petroleum products, a new high. Ras Tanura was the departure point for 80 percent of Aramco's exports in 1967, and liftings of crude oil and products exceeded 2 million barrels daily for the first time. • *Photo: unknown*

(◀) Saudi employees on company scholarships to Robert Morris College in Pittsburgh, Pennsylvania, take time from their studies to do a little sightseeing, 1962. From left are Omar Bataweel, Mohammed Hassan, Mohammed Saeed Al-Ali, Ali Dakheel Aburqubah, Saleh Al-Faleh and Abdulaziz Al-Abid.

These young men were among the 93 Saudi employees on educational and training assignments outside of the Kingdom that year. Today, from 500 to 700 students and trainees are enrolled each year in more than 100 North American colleges, universities and training facilities. • *Photo: unknown*

◀

'Abd al-Rahman Al-Barrak threads tape on a mainframe computer in January 1963. Al-Barrak became the first Saudi employee to qualify as a computer operator in September 1962. He started working for the company in 1952 as a payroll clerk and transferred to Computer Processing in 1961. He qualified as an operator of both the 4,000-unit and 16,000-unit IBM Model 1401 computers, used in processing company payrolls, financial and cost-accounting systems, personnel statistics and material supply records.
• *Photo: V.K. Antony*

▶

Employees receive instruction in basic and specialized manual skills in the Industrial Training Center facilities in Dhahran, December 1960. Enrollment in classes during working hours at the centers averaged 4,531 each trimester during the year. Two years later, the majority of students were experienced Saudi workmen taking specialized short courses in craft work such as bottom-hole testing, instrument applications, sketching and blueprint reading and electrical theory.

In 1960, Saudis made up slightly more than 75 percent of Aramco's workforce and 46 percent of them had been with the company 10 or more years. Seventy-six percent of the company's Saudi employees held semi-skilled, supervisory or professional jobs that year.
• *Photo: T.F. Walters*

Suwayyan Mas'ud pilots a Kenworth truck deep into the heart of the Rub' al-Khali, or Empty Quarter, part of a convoy transporting exploration teams. The journey from Dhahran to the exploration camp took eight days, at an average speed of 23 mph (37 kmh). The convoy consisted of nine tractor-trailers and four Dodge Power Wagons. One trailer carried a bulldozer, used to free stuck vehicles. One of the Power Wagons carried several live sheep, which were butchered and eaten along the way.
• Photo: T. Eigeland / Saudi Aramco World / PADIA

(◀)

Abdullah AbdulRahman, a rigman on a well in the Abu Sa'fah offshore field, carries away an old drilling bit after a new bit has been installed and the reassembling of the string has begun, August 1964. The Abu Sa'fah field, located 27 miles (43 km) northeast of Ras Tanura, was discovered in June of the previous year. In 2004, production of Arabian Medium crude oil from the Abu Sa'fah field was doubled, from 150,000 bpd to 300,000. • *Photo: V.K. Antony*

(▼)

In 1967, the company's 22 gas-oil separation plants (GOSPs) include Abqaiq GOSP-1, with a capacity of 215,000 barrels of crude oil daily. Production rose 8.6 percent over the previous year, and the 9 billionth barrel of crude flowed on November 22. The Berri field, discovered three years previously, also came on-stream.
• *Photo: S.M. Amin*

In a scene familiar to company employees for decades, traffic passes through the Dhahran Main Gate at 5 p.m., November 1966. The large gateway was built to commemorate an earlier royal visit. The main entrance to the company was relocated in the 1980s. This intersection today is busy with traffic heading toward the Research and Development Center, Westpark and Northpark office buildings and other facilities that have been built to keep pace with the company's growth. The small gatehouse in the left foreground was recently renovated to preserve a piece of Saudi Aramco history.
• *Photo: B.H. Moody*

Jamil Hattab hosts an episode of "Baba Hattab's Children's Story Time" on Aramco Television in May 1965. Hattab, an accomplished artist and an employee in Public Relations, created the show in 1958, and it was an instant hit with Eastern Province children and their parents. Each week, in a period costume of his own design, Baba Hattab, encircled by children, retold a tale from the *Arabian Nights*, highlighting the points to remember with his drawings, which flashed at intervals across the screen. Afterward, Baba Hattab would discuss the moral of the story with the children.

In 1965, the station was reaching an estimated audience of 350,000 viewers. "Baba Hattab's Children's Story Time" was telecast on Aramco's TV station until 1969. Jamil Hattab retired November 1, 1985. • *Photo: A.L. Yousif*

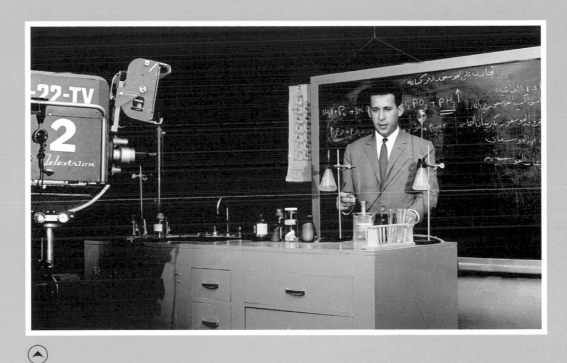

Science teacher Hashim Budayr of the Abqaiq Training Division conducts a chemistry experiment before studio cameras in March 1964. This special educational program was telecast daily from 10:30-11 a.m. by Aramco Channel 2 for Saudi Arabian Government Secondary School students in Dammam and Hofuf.

One-third of the Aramco station's air time was devoted to educational subjects. • *Photo: S.A. Ghamdi*

The finishing touches are put on the new home of Aramco employee Said Talib Makki, a supply control clerk in the general storehouse in Dhahran who purchased his home through the company's interest-free home loan program. By the end of 1961, when this photo was taken, more than 3,300 company employees had obtained homes through the company program.

Aramco was one of the few companies in the world to offer its employees interest-free home loans. Since 1951, the company's Home Ownership Program has issued loans to build more than 50,000 houses and has distributed over 15,000 free housing lots to Saudi employees. Today, prosperous-looking residential neighborhoods near established Saudi Aramco facilities are, for the most part, a result of the company's Home Ownership program. • *Photo: T.F. Walters*

1970 - 1979: Growth

1970

The offshore Berri field is brought on-stream.

Shipments of crude oil and petroleum products from the Ras Tanura Marine Terminal surpass 1 billion barrels a year for the first time.

1971

Crude oil production increases by more than 25 percent over 1970, averaging 4.5 million bpd.

1972

The fourth two-berth Sea Island loading facility is placed in service off Ras Tanura.

1973

The Saudi government acquires a 25-percent participation interest in Aramco.

1974

Tankers load at Ju'aymah, the newest Arabian Gulf oil-shipping terminal.

The Saudi Government increases its participation interest in the company to 60 percent.

Saudi Arabian desert in bloom, 1974 • Photo: K.A. Nasr

1975

The Saudi Government asks Aramco to design, build and operate the Master Gas System.

1976

Aramco becomes the only company in the world to produce more than 3 billion barrels of crude oil in a single calendar year.

1977

The Berri Gas Plant begins operations.

1978

The Qurayyah seawater treatment plant, the largest of its kind in the world, begins treating Arabian Gulf water for injection into oil fields.

1979

The port and industrial complex at Yanbu' Industrial City on the Red Sea, which includes several major company projects, is formally dedicated.

Workers inspect sections of enormous pipe, destined to deliver non-potable seawater to the northern Ghawar oil field to maintain reservoir pressure. This dual 56-inch and 60-inch pipeline, the largest in the company at the time, stretched 65 miles (105 km) from Qurayyah, south of Dhahran, to the injection area. This same year, 1974, saw 12 new water-injection facilities go on-stream, in the Berri field and the north 'Ain Dar and 'Uthmaniyah areas of Ghawar. Capacity increased by 3.2 million barrels per day for a total powered water-injection capacity of 9.3 million barrels of non-potable water. • *Photo: B.H. Moody*

His Majesty King Khalid ibn 'Abd al-'Aziz Al Sa'ud cuts the ribbon to officially commission the Berri NGL (natural gas liquids) Plant, October 29, 1977. To the right of His Majesty are H.E. Shaykh Ahmed Zaki Yamani, Minister of Petroleum and Mineral Resources, and Frank Jungers, Aramco Board Chairman and CEO. The Berri plant, originally designed as a gas collection and compression center, was modified to be the forerunner in basic design and principle for the Master Gas System and was the first of five major gas treatment plants to be completed. (Shedgum, 'Uthmaniyah, Ju'aymah and Yanbu' were the others, followed more recently by Hawiyah and Haradh.)

The Berri facility supplies fuel gas to the massive Jubail industrial complex – the cornerstone of which King Khalid laid before commissioning Berri – and NGL for export. In 2004, the gas-processing capacity of Berri was expanded to handle the additional volumes of gas produced as a result of the Qatif project, and the sulfur recovery units were upgraded to recover 99 percent of all sulfur. • *Photo: B.H. Moody*

A seismic charge erupts in the sand behind a company Hovercraft in a coastal zone north of Jubail on the Arabian Gulf in 1974. Conducting seismic work in the littoral, or tidal zones, had always presented a challenge. Conventional craft required 25 feet (7.6 m) of water at high tide to operate close to shore, and vehicles and men would flounder in the unstable conditions. The company turned to Hovercraft, which ride on a cushion of air, to gather its geophysical data in these areas. The unusual vessels operated as a team, with one setting the charge and the other acting as a recording unit.

Today, seismic work in these areas is carried out by "swamp buggies," tracked vehicles first developed to work in the swamps and marshes of Louisiana. • *Photo: S.M. Amin*

Personnel simulate an emergency escape from Safaniya gas-oil separation plant (GOSP) No. 3, employing a self-powered survival capsule, October 1977. The offshore Zuluf and Marjan fields, producing Arabian Medium crude oil, were reactivated this same year, with the construction of one onshore and two offshore GOSPs.

Aramco's first offshore GOSP was built in 1969 for the Safaniya field. Building the GOSPs offshore, close to the producing wells, raises the throughput capacity of the trunklines through which oil moves ashore and therefore increases the potential of offshore fields.
• *Photo: S.M. Amin*

The 540,000 deadweight ton (dwt) tanker *Batillus*, the world's largest at the time, loads 1.5 million barrels of crude oil, only 40 percent of its capacity, at one of the single-point moorings (SPM) at Ju'aymah, 1976. The Ju'aymah offshore terminal, 15 miles (24 km) northwest of Ras Tanura, opened in November 1974, with two SPMs in service with an initial shipping capacity of 1 million barrels of crude per day.

Today, there are six SPMs, five active and one on standby, and tankers ranging from 150,000 to 750,000 dwt load oil through flexible cargo hoses connecting ships to the SPMs, which are connected to metering platforms via sub-sea lines of sizes up to 48 inches in diameter. • *Photo: S.M. Amin*

A cross section of the people of Aramco pose in Ras Tanura for the cover of the 1973 annual review. The wide range of occupations in the company is represented by the presence in the portrait of engineers, plant superintendents, geologists, surveyors, accountants, harbor pilots, chemists, surgeons, managers, teachers, secretaries, nurses, draftsmen, airplane pilots, firemen, photographers, radio operators and apprentices.

At the end of 1973, there were 13,001 employees, of whom 79 percent were Saudi nationals and about 9 percent were Americans. Of the 738 total supervisory positions, Saudis occupied 297 of them, an increase of 18.3 percent over the previous year.
• Photo: B.H. Moody

Every summer, Saudi Aramco employs Saudi college and university students in a wide variety of departments. The students, who are attending schools around the world and inside the Kingdom, gain practical work experience, and many of them join the company full time after graduation. In this photo, taken in Dhahran in 1975 when 198 students participated in the program, three students from the University of Petroleum and Minerals work in a laboratory for the Production Engineering Division. Left to right are Usamah Kamakhi, a senior in chemical engineering, Husni Nahhas and Saad Al-Turaiki, BS graduates in chemical engineering. Thirty years later — a career span not uncommon for the company, whether Saudi or expatriate — Al-Turaiki was still with the company, in the position of Executive Director, Southern Area Gas Operations.
• *Photo: unknown*

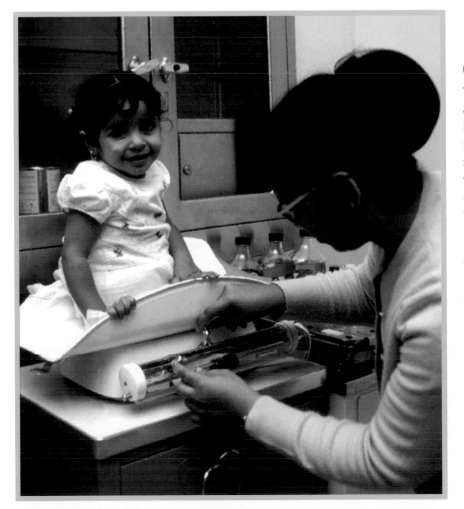

The daughter of a Saudi employee is weighed as part of her regular check-up, provided free by the company as part of its health-care package for employees. All employees, and some 45,000 dependents of Saudi employees, were covered by the company's free medical care and health protection programs in 1971, when this photo was taken at the Dhahran Health Center.

The previous year, Aramco's Medical Department cooperated with the government to combat cholera by inoculating virtually all Saudi employees and dependents over the course of three weekends.

On a typical day in the early part of the decade, nearly 2,000 people visited company clinics.
• *Photo: A.M. Al-Khalifa*

▶

This local firm, a manufacturer of paper products and plastic bags, is one of 35 Saudi firms employing 3,200 men receiving technical assistance from Aramco's Local Industrial Development Department in 1970. Other businesses that benefited from the company's support this year were a cold storage and meat processing plant in Dammam, a radiator factory, and a private electric power company. The firms receiving assistance produced revenues of about $30 million. Aramco also paved streets and installed curbs and sidewalks in al-Khobar, and drilled a water well in Dammam.
• *Photo: S.M. Al-Ghamdi*

▼

Research began in 1970 to determine how well sugar beets would perform under local conditions, and the results, seen in the photo below from 1974, with Aramco's Sami A. Labban on the right, were encouraging.

In that same year, vegetable production increased by 2.6 million pounds (1.2 million kg) to about 17 million pounds (7.7 million kg). Egg production reached 37.5 million and broiler chicken production grew to 1.2 million.

About 1,000 families benefited through employment by farmers and agricultural supply agencies, earning $13.7 million, nearly $2 million more than the year before. • *Photo: S.M. Amin*

Agriculture might not seem to be any concern of an oil company, but from its very beginnings, Aramco found itself caught up in the development not only of an industry, but of a country as well. The transfer of knowledge and expertise by the company across a wide spectrum of fields, from farming to roads, and from health care to manufacturing, represents one of Aramco's greatest legacies to the people of Saudi Arabia.

Saudi girls play during recess at their Aramco-built government school in the town of al-Khobar in 1973, the 46th such facility built by the company to that point. Aramco not only builds the schools, it also pays for the costs of operation and maintenance. Through 1973, the company had spent nearly $53 million including construction and operation and maintenance costs.

Three decades later, the number of company-built government schools had surpassed 135, almost equally divided between boys and girls.
• *Photo: B.H. Moody*

◀

Originally serialized in 14 issues of *Aramco World* magazine beginning in 1968, *Discovery!* tells the story of the company's early days, from the events leading up to the signing of the original concession in 1933 through February 1945, when seven American wives, exiled by World War II, returned to Dhahran.

The company commissioned well-known American writer Wallace Stegner (1909-1993) to tell the story of how the people of two different cultures surmounted enormous challenges and together created the foundation for the world's largest oil producing and exporting enterprise.

Stegner, who founded the prestigious creative writing program at Stanford University, went on to win the 1971 Pulitzer Prize for *Angle of Repose* and the 1976 National Book Award for *The Spectator Bird*.

The paperback edition pictured here was printed in Beirut in 1971.

▶

Students walk to class on the campus of the College of Petroleum and Minerals in April 1970, the same year Aramco agreed to contribute more than $14 million to the school's expansion program. The following year, the university issued its first degrees.

In 1975, the College of Petroleum and Minerals became the University of Petroleum and Minerals, and in 1986, the university was renamed The King Fahd University of Petroleum and Minerals.

The company and the university have always had a mutually beneficial relationship, with the company supporting the school in a variety of ways and many of the students coming to work after graduation.

The college, established by Royal Decree in September 1963, first admitted students in 1964. Since then, more than 8,575 degrees have been awarded and enrollment has grown from an initial class of 67 to more than 10,000.
• Photo: B.H. Moody

A 500-ton pressure column, the largest one-item move the company had done up to that time, moves down the road to Abqaiq as part of the expansion of its NGL facilities. In the spring of 1975, three enormous columns arrived by ship from Japan. One column, 126 feet (38 m) long and weighing 400 tons, was placed in the Ras Tanura Refinery.

The other two vessels, one weighing 420 tons and measuring 140 feet (43 m) in length (the 500-ton model was 110 feet/34 m long), were delivered to Abqaiq one at a time, pulled by a 700-horsepower Kenworth Dart truck, one of the most powerful trucks in the world.

The journey from Ras Tanura to Abqaiq took four days. The columns were placed on two trailers with a combined total of 192 wheels. Two men can be seen riding on the rear of the last trailer. One man actually steered the trailer and the other controlled the hydraulic system. • *Photo: A.G. Dhaghish*

A young visitor to Aramco's Mobile Oil Exhibit gazes up at the ceiling of the central tent at the road show's final performance under canvas, in the town of Marakh, 1972. The traveling exhibit toured the Kingdom 50 times in the course of 14 years, hosting some 1.5 million Saudi visitors. The exhibit consisted of four sections: a central rotunda with a scale model of a drilling rig and three rectangular pavilions housing a science exhibit, "The Story of Oil," and the traditional and modern faces of the Kingdom.

The idea of a mobile exhibit can be traced back to September 1954, when the Saudi government asked Aramco to participate in a trade exposition in Damascus, Syria. The company later staged exhibitions in Cairo in 1959 and 1965 in coordination with Tapline. The first time exhibit materials were put on view in Saudi Arabia was in the spring of 1955, when the company responded to a request for a contribution to a school exhibit in Makkah.

The mobile exhibit remained open in villages for two to three weeks at a time, and for twice that long in larger cities, introducing the citizens of the country to its most important natural resource and the industry developing it. The "big top" version of the exhibit, weighing 45 tons and packed in 130 crates and boxes, was retired in favor of a specially-designed van. Aramco donated the tent to the Red Crescent Society for use as a health services clinic for pilgrims during hajj. • *Photo: K.A. Nasr / Saudi Aramco World / PADIA*

⊙

In 1972, 65 Saudi university students and recent graduates were enrolled in the summer program, among them Faruk Kunash, far right, and Ahmad Hakami, both working in the survey unit of the Engineering Department. Hakami had recently graduated with a bachelor's in civil engineering, and Kunash was working toward the same degree.
• *Photo: S. Al-Ghamdi*

⊙

Students from an advanced machinery maintenance course assist with the disassembly of a turbine and compressor during a test-and-inspection shutdown at the Ras Tanura hydroformer. Right to left are Traheeb Al-Jurais, instructor Floyd McGinnis, Lahoom Nassir, Ibrahim al-Shrawey and Ameer Al-Momin.

These students were among the approximately 875 Saudi employees receiving job-related training in 1970. Aramco offered specialized courses in its technical curriculum in machinery maintenance, advanced electricity and electronic instrumentation. The courses ranged in length from 10 to 15 months.
• *Photo: S. Al-Ghamdi*

⊙

The world calls for energy at Ras Tanura Sea Island Terminal and, in the middle distance, the North Pier, 1974. In the background is the tank farm, where three storage tanks, each with a capacity of more than 1 million barrels, were completed the year before.

In December of 1972, the fourth Sea Island was completed, adding two more berths for tankers.

These are just a handful of the 4,470 ships that called at Aramco's Arabian Gulf terminals during the year, loading almost 2.9 billion barrels of crude oil and refined products. • Photo: B.H. Moody

⊙

Ahmad Kudaisi, an Aramco harbor pilot, issues a command over his radio as he guides a tanker ship to its berth at Ras Tanura's North Pier. Company harbor pilots, like their counterparts in every port and inland waterway the world over, are responsible for berthing and unberthing ships that call at company terminals in the Gulf and the Red Sea.

The successful shipment of crude oil from company facilities rests in large part upon the skills of the harbor pilots, who, as the first person aboard ships calling from around the globe, must act as ambassadors for the company and the Kingdom. Harbor pilots must also win the trust of the ship's master and crew and demonstrate thorough professionalism.

In 1970, when this photo was taken, 3,170 tankers called at the port of Ras Tanura, loading more than 3 million barrels a day, making this the first year more than 1 billion barrels of oil were shipped from Ras Tanura. In 2004, there were 47 harbor pilots, nearly all of whom were Saudi nationals at various stages in their careers. • Photo: T. Eigeland / Saudi Aramco World / PADIA

Seawater rushes through the intake channel at the Qurayyah seawater treatment plant. Completed in 1978, the plant, the world's largest, initially supplied 4.2 million barrels per day of treated seawater, replacing saline aquifer water for injection in the Ghawar field to maintain reservoir pressure. In November 2005, in conjunction with a host of enormous projects to increase crude oil production capacity, the capacity of the Qurayyah facility was also increased, to 9 million barrels per day, with plans to expand it a further 4.2 million barrels per day by the end of the decade.

Water from the Gulf flows through an intake channel into a structure where it is screened and chlorinated. From there, it is piped to an above-ground canal at the treatment plant, 1,500 feet (457 m) inland from the Gulf. There, treatment modules filter and deoxygenate the water to remove suspended solids and dissolved oxygen to suitable levels. The treated seawater is then pumped via pipelines to 'Uthmaniyah where it is distributed to water-injection pump stations.

Water is pumped into the subsurface producing reservoir below the oil-water contact area and helps maintain pressure by moving into the oil zone behind the oil and gas that are produced. At the same time, the water sweeps the oil ahead of it toward the producing wells. • *Photo: S.M. Amin / Saudi Aramco World / PADIA*

Aramco's main computer banks in 1974 store data on magnetic tapes and are connected to other company areas by 184 remote terminals. Computers arrived at Aramco in the 1940s in the form of electrical tabulating machines. A decade later, the first mainframe computers were put into service processing payrolls, financial data, personnel statistics and materials supply records.

Three decades later, computer data storage in the Exploration and Petroleum Engineering Center's Computer Center alone reached 1.2 petabytes (about 1.2 million gigabytes). The computer banks in the Exploration and Petroleum Engineering Center's Computer Center have long since evolved into PC clusters of thousands of processors, capable of performing more than 1.65 trillion floating point operations per second.
• *Photo: S.M. Amin*

In 1977, Aramco had three of the largest projects in the world going at one time: the Master Gas System; the offshore Zuluf GOSP-2, completed late in the year; and the Qurayyah Seawater Treatment Plant.

The decade of the 1970s witnessed perhaps the biggest growth in company operations since the post-World War II boom. Three areas in particular drove the expansion: a program to increase the company's crude production capacity; the Master Gas System; and management of the Saudi Consolidated Electric Company's (SCECO) power generation, transmission and distribution program in the Eastern Province.

In the first four years of the decade, average daily crude production leapt from 3.5 million barrels per day (bpd) to 8.2 million bpd.

The construction programs stretched the company's infrastructure to its limits as the workforce rose by more than 27 percent in 1977. Evidence of the company's rapid expansion in the mid-1970s is this "floating hotel" used to house contractor construction workers at Ju'aymah in 1977.

This five-story accommodation barge, built in Japan and sailed to Aramco, was one of four in use by the end of the year. The four floating hotels, each with its own generators, desalination facilities, air-conditioning, dining halls and recreation areas, housed a total of 4,500 contractor workers. An additional 37,900 bachelors and 875 families lived on expanded temporary camps. • *Photo: S.M. Amin*

▲ Process engineers in Houston, Texas, in the mid-1970s assemble a model of the gas-treating module for the Natural Gas Liquification Plant, part of the Shedgum Gas Plant. The Berri Gas Plant was the first plant to be completed as part of the Master Gas System, with two other gas plants at Shedgum and 'Uthmaniyah becoming fully operational in 1981 and 1982, respectively.

In 1975, the Saudi Government unveiled a five-year development plan and called upon Aramco to design, develop and operate a gas-gathering and processing system to supply fuel for a vast new industrial network. Known as the Master Gas System, the project — one of the largest engineering and construction projects ever undertaken by an oil company — would gather and treat associated gas and then ship it via pipelines to complexes to fuel aluminum smelters, steel mills, petrochemical plants, water-desalination plants and electrical generators, as well as provide liquid gas for export.

The engineering phase of the Master Gas System alone employed some 2,500 engineers and craftsmen and would take nearly 200 million man-hours to complete. • *Photo: K. Thomas / Saudi Aramco World / PADIA*

▶ Hydrocarbon products are tested for total sulfur content in the Ras Tanura Laboratory in this undated photograph from the 1970s. The lab began operations in 1944 to serve the Ras Tanura Refinery. In April 1997, the laboratory moved into a state-of-the-art facility and today serves as the quality control and technical support laboratory for Ras Tanura Refinery, responsible for crude oil royalty testing and shipment release testing of other petroleum products.

Other customers for the lab include Ju'aymah gas plant (liquefied petroleum gas products); Ras Tanura Marine Terminals (export products); the Environmental Protection Department; and bulk plants and tank farms that distribute finished products to the local market.

Lab personnel take some 12,000 samples and perform around 38,000 tests every month. In early 2004, the lab earned its ISO 9001:2000 re-certification, making it the only laboratory in Saudi Aramco and in the Gulf Cooperation Council (GCC) to achieve this level of excellence. • *Photo: S.M. Amin*

▲

An Aramco biologist cradles a baby sea turtle, one of four species found in the Arabian Gulf, just one of many plant and animal species surveyed in a five-year company study of the Arabian Gulf and its Saudi Arabian shores. The survey's findings were published in 1977 in a 285-page, superbly illustrated book titled *Biotopes of the Western Arabian Gulf: Marine Life and Environments of Saudi Arabia*.

The volume includes, among many other things, a 65-page species list of the animals and plants inhabiting the Gulf, more than half of them never before reported there.

The impetus for the survey was the mounting tempo of petroleum production and shipping in the Gulf, along with increased industrialization. Farsighted officials of the Saudi Arabian Government and executives from Aramco saw the need to establish a biological baseline of plant and animal life in the Gulf, a norm against which any future ecological changes could be measured.
• *Photo: unknown*

1980 - 1989: Transformation

1980

The government increases its participation interest in Aramco's crude oil concession rights, production and facilities to 100 percent, with retroactive financial effect to 1976.

1981

Data processing begins at the EXPEC (Exploration and Petroleum Engineering Center) Computer Center, one of the world's largest geoscience computing facilities.

Shedgum Gas Plant becomes fully operational.

1982

The discovery well, Dammam No. 7, is shut in after producing almost 32.5 million barrels of oil over 45 years.

'Uthmaniyah Gas Plant and the Ju'aymah Fractionation Plant and Marine Export Terminal go on-stream.

1983

Ali I. Al-Naimi is the first Saudi appointed company president, effective January 1984.

The Ras Tanura Port Control Center is inaugurated.

1984

The company resumes operation of the East-West Crude Oil Pipeline.

The company's shipping subsidiary, Vela International Marine Ltd., is founded.

East-West Pipeline, 1985 • Photo: S.M. Amin

1985
Non-associated gas capacity reaches 1 billion standard cubic feet per day (scfd).

1986
A 250,000 bpd crude oil distillation unit, an asphalt plant and a sulfur-recovery unit are commissioned at Ras Tanura Refinery.

A sulfur-pelletizing and export facility opens at Jubail Industrial Port.

1987
The East-West Crude Oil Pipeline capacity is expanded to 3.2 million bpd.

The new Aramco Exhibit opens in Dhahran.

1988
The Saudi Arabian Oil Company (Saudi Aramco) is established.

A company subsidiary and Texaco establish the company's first joint refining and marketing venture, Star Enterprise, in the eastern and Gulf Coast U.S.

1989
The first oil discoveries in central Saudi Arabia — at Hawtah and Dilam, south of Riyadh — are announced.

An employee uses an IBM 7350 Advanced Image Processing Systems (AIPS), one of four installed in the EXPEC (Exploration and Petroleum Engineering Center) Computer Center in 1983, the first full year of operations for the Center. A prototype of the computer had been installed the previous year. It proved so successful that IBM asked for permission to display software produced by Aramco using the 7350 at the annual convention of the Society of Exploration Geophysicists.

The first of its kind in the Middle East, EXPEC not only served to develop and implement exploration technology and better manage reservoirs, it became an incubator of Saudi geoscientists, petroleum engineers and technicians. • *Photo: unknown*

The scale of industrial projects in the Kingdom during the early 1980s is apparent from this pipe yard in Yanbu' in 1982. Two sleepy towns — Jubail, on the Gulf Coast, and Yanbu' on the Red Sea — were transformed into giant industrial cities as part of a government plan to restructure the Kingdom's oil-export economy. New hydrocarbon industries were built in both cities: petroleum refining, gas treatment and processing, and petrochemical plants.

Supplied with crude and natural gas liquids by the East-West pipeline, the Saudi Aramco crude oil terminal and NGL fractionation plant are two of the leading industries in Yanbu'.

The crude oil terminal in Yanbu' was built in 1982 by Petromin and integrated into Aramco in 1984. The terminal includes four tanker-loading berths and a crude oil tank farm with a capacity of 12.5 million barrels. Ships taking on cargo at Yanbu' for Europe or North America can save about 4,000 nautical miles (7,400 kilometers) per round trip, compared with sailing around the Arabian Peninsula to the Kingdom's Eastern Province terminals.
• *Photo: T. Eigeland / Saudi Aramco World / PADIA*

◀

Fin-fan coolers, atop one of the twin gas-fractionation modules of the Ju'aymah Gas Plant, stretch into the distance, 1988. The module's de-ethanizer column is in the foreground. Ju'aymah Gas Plant is a critical component of the Master Gas System, producing ethane feedstock for industrial customers at Jubail, and propane, butane and natural gasoline for export. • *Photo: S.M. Amin*

▼

An operator at 'Uthmaniyah Gas Plant watches over the processing and distribution of gas on his automated control system in the mid-1980s. Gas-processing facilities at Berri, Shedgum, 'Uthmaniyah and Hawiyah treat the gas and recover natural gas liquids (NGL). Gas is delivered to the sales gas distribution grid, and NGL is sent to fractionation plants at Ju'aymah and Yanbu'. These plants supply petrochemical feedstock and liquefied petroleum gas (LPG) for export and local industrial consumption.

The Master Gas System, one of the largest engineering and construction projects ever undertaken by an oil company, today handles more than 9 billion standard cubic feet of gas every day. At the end of 2004, gas reserves stood at 237 trillion standard cubic feet, placing Saudi Arabia fourth in the world in reserves.
• *Photo: unknown*

The Aramco Board of Directors, in its meeting on November 8, 1983, decided that Ali I. Al-Naimi, seated at right, would be the president of Aramco effective January 1, 1984, becoming the first Saudi president of the company. In many ways, Al-Naimi's career symbolizes the growth of the company and of the Kingdom.

Al-Naimi came to Aramco as an illiterate Bedouin boy, attended the company's Jabal School and in 1947 was hired as a junior clerk in Personnel. Sponsored by the company, he attended the American University in Beirut and later earned a bachelor's degree in geology at Lehigh University in the United States in 1962 and a master's in geology from Stanford in 1963. He later completed the Executive Program in Business Administration at Columbia University and the Advanced Management Program at Harvard. In August 1995, Al-Naimi was appointed Minister of Petroleum and Mineral Resources. • *Photo: N.S.C.*

Work to expand the East-West crude oil pipeline continues into the twilight hours in the rugged terrain in western Saudi Arabia, 1986. Four years previously, two pipelines were completed linking oil-production facilities in the Eastern Province with Yanbu'. One line transports natural gas liquids (NGL) from gas-processing facilities at Shedgum 727 miles (1,170 km) distant. The other pipeline, 746 miles (1,200 km) long, delivers crude oil from Abqaiq. The two pipelines are the most advanced computer-monitored hydrocarbons pipelines ever built.

The crude oil pipeline, 48 inches (122 cm) in diameter, was initially able to deliver 1.85 million bpd to Yanbu' for refining or export. The company, which formally took on the operation of the crude oil line in 1984, expanded capacity to 3.2 million bpd by laying a parallel string of 56-inch (142-cm) pipe connected to the existing stations. An additional pumping system in late 1992 increased capacity to 5 million bpd. • *Photos: S.M. Amin*

▶

One of more than 1,900 employees to attend technical and vocational training programs in 1987 makes adjustments to a gleaming circuit board in the Abqaiq craft skills electrical training shop. Approximately 7,700 employees received job-related academic training during the year. The company's training program, one of the largest of its type in the world, was staffed by about 1,720 full-time teachers, instructors and support personnel operating at five main Industrial Training Centers, five Job Skills Training Centers and four Satellite Training Centers. The number of Saudi employees in higher education reflected the success of Aramco's emphasis on training and continuing education, with 734 Saudis studying for bachelor's degrees and 23 working toward graduate degrees. • *Photo: S.M. Amin*

▼

Firemen at the Dhahran training ground in 1984 battle a blaze similar to one they might encounter at one of the company's oil or gas installations. During the year, four Aramco fire-fighting facilities were completed. Formalized safety training was provided to a record number of more than 8,000 employees, and the industrial lost-time frequency rate neared a historical low of 0.30 per 200,000 man-hours worked.

An Advanced Fire Training Center, located near Ras Tanura, began offering classes in 2005. One of the most sophisticated training facilities in the world, the center includes a variety of firefighting scenarios: an integrated process complex, a tank farm and a structural complex that can also be used for marine firefighting scenarios, all of which are designed to simulate a variety of fires in a supervised, controlled situation. • *Photo: S.M. Amin*

◀

A new atmospheric column, weighing 690 metric tons and measuring 256 feet (77.9 m) high, is lifted into position at the Ras Tanura Refinery in 1985. A second column, weighing 719 metric tons and measuring 185 feet (56.3 m) high, was also erected, both part of a 250,000-bpd two-stage crude distillation unit built for the greater Ras Tanura Refinery modernization project. Also completed during the year was a plant designed to extract 300 metric tons of elemental sulfur per day from waste gas.

Even in the midst of the extensive modernization project, the refinery processed 411,000 bpd of crude oil. The NGL fractionation plant at the refinery, and two others at Ju'aymah and Yanbu', processed large volumes of propane, butane and natural gasoline.
• *Photo: M.J. Isaac*

▼

A company employee in safety gear sandblasts one of three 600,000-barrel tanks at the 6 million barrel natural gas liquids (NGL) fractionation plant tank farm at Yanbu' on the Red Sea, 1988. The work was part of a test and inspection of 11 large crude oil storage tanks and 10 NGL product-storage tanks erected earlier in the decade. The NGL plant at Yanbu' is one of three such company plants (the other two are at Ju'aymah and Ras Tanura on the Gulf coast). Together, the three plants processed 171,000 bpd of propane, 106,000 bpd of butane and 62,000 bpd of natural gasoline in 1988. The grand total of all NGL for the year was 126 million barrels, most of which was for export. By 2003, the export figure had more than doubled to 266 million barrels. • *Photo: I. Bennett*

◀

The enormous scale of Aramco's operations requires a diligent maintenance staff, adept in a wide variety of skills. Here, a technician inspects the slots of a large stator (the housing for a motor) in the Dhahran electrical shops, 1982. In this year alone, technicians, mechanics and other support services personnel maintained 467 buses, 10,230 sedans and other light vehicles, plus a fleet of fire trucks, ambulances and deep-desert vehicles.

Exploration and producing attract the lion's share of attention, but this same year, the company also overlaid 180 miles (290 km) of public and company roads with hot asphalt, built 10 miles (16 km) of new and upgraded roads and performed site preparation at 708 well locations. New office buildings involved office moves for 9,000 personnel. To ensure the maintenance work force remained best in class, maintenance training facilities were completed in Dhahran, Ju'aymah and Shedgum to handle 440 trainees per year.
• *Photo: S.M. Amin*

(▲)

His Majesty King Fahd ibn 'Abd al-'Aziz Al Sa'ud, the Custodian of the Two Holy Mosques, waves to the crowd as he and HRH Crown Prince Abd 'Allah prepare to depart after attending the opening ceremony of the Exploration and Petroleum Engineering Center, or EXPEC, and its associated computer center and laboratories, May 16, 1983. His Majesty's visit also marked the 50th anniversary of the company, dating back to the concession signing of May 29, 1933. • *Photo: J. Champney*

(▶)

A young girl improves her motor and cognitive skills through play, part of a therapy program at the Dhahran Health Center, 1988. The 11 company clinics handled almost 1.3 million patient visits during the year. Improvements in patient care included the use of Doppler ultrasonography equipment and a nuclear medicine Rota camera to advance the physicians' ability to diagnose abnormalities in blood vessels and organs, including the heart. A computerized laboratory system was installed to improve the processing of lab tests, 2.2 million of which are carried out annually.

Saudi employees entered the medical profession in greater numbers in 1988, with 17 specialty doctors, 36 general practitioners, 10 dentists and 34 medical and dental technicians involved in professional training.
• *Photo: S.M. Amin*

▲

Avid young readers have their imaginations fueled during a visit to one of Aramco's mobile libraries in the mid-1980s. The Mobile Library Program was launched in 1982 in coordination with the Directorate General of Education to provide educational services for elementary school students. Today, nine well-equipped trailers reach more than 100,000 students in more than 100 schools throughout the Kingdom every year. Each visitor can check out two books for a two-week period.

Since its inception, the mobile libraries have visited more than 1,900 schools and distributed some 900,000 books to 450,000 students.
• *Photo: S.M. Amin*

▲

A local farmer reaps a bounty of tilapia from a fish farm, one of several established with advice from Aramco aquaculture specialists. The fish-farming project in al-Hasa demonstrated how to harness excess irrigation drainage water to raise fish, helping farmers produce a valuable food source and earn extra income.

Aramco continued its long tradition of assisting local communities and new businesses in the Eastern Province, cooperating with the Ministry of Agriculture on a wide range of projects.

At Aramco's 300-acre (120-hectare) al-Hasa Demonstration Farm, 15 new varieties of vegetables were cultivated on a trial basis. Extension Services distributed these same varieties to local farmers and also encouraged them to install underground drainage systems to improve soil fertility. • *Photo: S.M. Amin*

Aramco biologists check a seine net in Tarut Bay to determine the potential of commercial fishing, 1986. This marked the second year of joint studies with the King Fahd University of Petroleum and Minerals' Research Institute on the ecosystem of Tarut Bay.

This same year witnessed the completion of a three-year ecological study of Manifa and Tanajib bays. Another project, the Abqaiq Greenbelt, a 131-acre (53-hectare) plot between a new highway and the Abqaiq home ownership area, watered with treated wastewater from the company-run sewage treatment plant, protected nearby homes from wind and sand movement and beautified the landscape.

Three years later, the company assisted in the publication of the most complete work ever printed on the birds of the western Gulf and its hinterlands: *Birds of the Eastern Province of Saudi Arabia*, a volume that covered 340 species. • *Photo: S.M. Amin*

A company scuba diver helps carry out a study on a reef system near company installations in this undated photograph from the 1980s. Coral reefs are some of the most sensitive ecosystems on the planet and the company monitors reef systems near company operations in the Red Sea and the Gulf for impact.

Saudi Aramco has been implementing environmental programs for decades. The company has developed a broad array of environmental requirements, engineering standards and guidelines to implement its stringent environmental policy, including sanitary codes, project environmental assessments, air quality and emission standards, noise control regulations, landfill standards, water recycling procedures, oil spill contingency plans and hazardous material disposal rules.

The company also assesses the environmental impact of its operations, studies the marine environment and protection of groundwater resources and has also launched environmental research projects and studies in collaboration with national universities and private organizations. Many of Saudi Aramco's employees devote time to environmental activities such as the community recycling program, and tree and mangrove planting projects. A large proportion of the public areas in Dhahran are irrigated with tertiary-treated wastewater, in a program that has saved billions of gallons of precious groundwater.
• *Photo: unknown*

Hesham Najiya of the Dhahran Cubs swings and misses as catcher Mike Bissell and umpire Al De Jesus wait for the ball, June 1988. Baseball has always been popular in company communities, and its Little League teams have done particularly well. The Arabian American Little League was founded in 1986, and its traveling team is composed of all-stars from teams in Dhahran, Ras Tanura, Abqaiq and al-Khobar. In 2005, the team went undefeated in the European tournament and advanced to its 17th appearance in the Little League World Series in Williamsport, Pennsylvania. • *Photo: N.S.C.*

Fahad al-Ahmed dribbles around an opponent while Kenny Ostrowski follows, July 1988. These boys belong to the Aramco Youth Soccer Organization, one of the most popular recreation clubs in company communities. Employees in all communities participate in a wide variety of activities such as golf, tennis, squash, swimming, cricket, softball, basketball, running, volleyball, bicycling, badminton, scuba diving, sailing, horse riding, weightlifting, and aerobics, among others, all organized by self-directed groups and with access to excellent facilities.
• *Photo: I. Bennett*

Children frolic on a playground at the company beach on the Arabian Gulf not far from Dhahran, 1988. With the collapse of oil prices in the mid-1980s, the company downsized, shedding 17,000 positions, its total workforce declining from more than 60,000 in 1982 to 43,500 in 1987. Still, there were nearly 20,000 people living in the six residential communities in 1988.
• *Photo: S.M. Amin*

Participants in a management training seminar exchange ideas, Dhahran, November 1987. The process of identifying high-potential Saudis and developing their capabilities through training programs, schooling and job assignments began in the 1940s. By combining in-house training with regional and international courses — and more recently, with distance and e-learning courses — Aramco's management has developed the skills necessary to guide the company through the challenges posed by seminal events such as the government's purchase of the company, Saudization, downstream investments, globalization and strategic alliances.

By the end of the decade, Saudis held nearly all of the company's top management positions, 76 percent of the supervisory positions, 77 percent of the industrial jobs and about 60 percent of the professional positions — testament to the company's commitment to nurturing leadership from within. • *Photo: S.M. Amin*

The distinctive stained-glass windows and minaret of the Dhahran Mosque glow at sunset. • *Photo: S.M. Amin*

An aerial view of the Dhahran headquarters complex, January 1989. Two months before, on November 8, 1988, Saudi Aramco was created by Royal Decree. The Saudi government had begun to purchase Aramco's assets from its shareholders — Standard Oil of California and Texaco (today's Chevron Corporation), Exxon and Mobil (now ExxonMobil) — in 1973. The acquisition was completed in 1980 and retroactive to 1976, although Aramco continued to operate and manage the Kingdom's oil fields for the government.

The original U-shaped administration building, now backed by two square annex buildings, each enclosing a courtyard, can be seen in the right of the photo. The Tower Administration building is centered between the older admin complex on the right and the Exploration and Petroleum Engineering Center, or EXPEC, and Engineering complex on the left. In the foreground, at left, is the Dhahran community commissary and at right, the triangular Al-Mujamma' community services center. In the center of the photo is the Dhahran Mosque. • *Photo: S.M. Amin*

As dusk falls, the thorny branches of an acacia tree frame the lights of Well No. 1 at Hawtah, 118 miles (190 km) south of Riyadh, September 1989. In June, a high gravity, sweet crude oil was discovered at around 6,234 feet (1,900 m) in this well and, in October, new oil and gas zones were discovered at a site 47 miles (75 km) southeast of Riyadh near ad-Dilam.

Two years previously, the company embarked on the largest exploration program ever undertaken in the Kingdom. The strikes at Hawtah and ad-Dilam were the first discoveries resulting from the exploration campaign. Five seismic crews were at work during the year in the first forays outside the original retained areas in the northern, central and southern areas of the country, covering an average of 398 seismic line-miles (640 line-km) per month.
• *Photo: R.H. Al-Laif*

Mechanical engineer Khalid Al-Faddagh, on assignment in 1989 at a turbo-machinery firm in Pennsylvania in the United States, gains insights about equipment vital to company gas and refining operations. Al-Faddagh headed a variety of company projects involving compressors and rotating equipment before taking up his year-long posting in the United States. Al-Faddagh later earned a doctorate in mechanical engineering from the Imperial College of London, and in 2003, was named president of Petron, Saudi Aramco's equity venture in the Philippines.

Like many company employees sent on overseas assignments, he was able to strengthen his expertise in his field and broaden his experiences, a valuable asset as Saudi Aramco expanded its international operations throughout the late 1980s. Saudi Aramco employees were working and living in the United States, Europe and the Far East, conduits for the exchange of technical and cultural knowledge. • *Photo: H.H.*

Cartographer Abdul-Ghani Al-Humud checks a three-dimensional stratigraphic model depicting the porosity of an offshore oil reservoir, Dhahran, September 1989. The computer-generated model is based on digital data recorded by instruments inserted deep into well bores.

In a new development, well-log data, combined with X-ray diffraction, were used to identify and correlate reservoir rock facies. This information generated graphic depictions of the distribution of reservoir rocks, enhancing reservoir development and planning.

Such technological developments were made possible by the rapid increases made in computer processor speeds and memory storage, and by the efforts of company personnel in the Exploration and Petroleum Engineering Center, or EXPEC. The Center, which links computer, exploration, petroleum engineering and laboratory facilities, essentially eliminated the company's dependence on upstream technological support from other oil companies.
• *Photo: S.M. Amin*

A geologist examines a core sample, looking to unlock the story of an oil or gas field. Core samples provide the only hands-on contact with the component rocks and fluids of hydrocarbon reservoirs. Geologists can gauge the porosity and permeability of the reservoir and help answer critical questions such as: Which reservoirs are most promising? How much oil or gas is in the reservoir? What percent of the oil and gas reserves are recoverable?

A new facility for core handling opened in Dhahran in 1982, seven years before this photo was taken. The facility underwent renovation in 1994. Most recently, the entire process of core handling, from the well site to the lab, was re-engineered, and the facility, officially titled the Well Samples and Laboratory Unit, is one of the finest in the world. The facility also serves as an archive for core samples, that, if laid end to end, would stretch more than 150 miles (241 km). • *Photo: S.M. Amin*

A company geoscientist analyzes a computer-enhanced satellite image of the Kingdom's surface, looking for anomalies that might be expressions of subsurface structures, 1989. Satellite imagery such as this, taken from a Landsat satellite from an orbit some 435 miles (700 km) above the Earth, has replaced pictures taken from single-engine planes. The company, and the industry, had come a long way from the Fairchild 71 days.

Aircraft were, and still are, used to conduct aerial magnetic surveys to measure the earth's magnetic variations to help discern possible hydrocarbon-bearing formations. In 1989, geoscientists completed preliminary interpretation of approximately 50,000 miles (80,000 km) of aerial magnetic surveys flown the year before. • *Photo: S.M. Amin*

▲

Automated cranes, directed by a microcomputer system, place and retrieve medical materials in a company supply storehouse, 1989. The use of computers rapidly expanded throughout the company in the 1980s. A three-year worldwide computer consolidation program that condensed seven installations and eight different computers into a single computer system reached completion in 1989. The company installed more than 650 new computer workstations during the year and an on-line inventory control system. • *Photo: S.M. Amin*

▲

Harbor Pilot Mohammed Yones radios commands to the tugs gently maneuvering a tanker into position, 1989. Pilots use a combination of current, wind and tug power to berth the enormous tankers. The tug on the bow is more than 900 feet (274 m) away, and Yones, on his perch on the wing of the bridge, is nearly 200 feet (60 m) above the surface of the Gulf. This tanker was one of 2,134 vessels that called at company export terminals in 1989, the 50th anniversary of the export of Saudi crude oil to world markets. • *Photo: S.M. Amin*

A field geologist examines rock in October 1989, part of an exploration campaign covering 579,153 square miles (1.5 million sq km), a region larger than Germany, France and Spain combined. In the five years between 1989 and 1994, Saudi Aramco discovered 15 oil and gas fields in the central and northwestern parts of the Kingdom and on the Red Sea Coast. This expanded exploration work was the result of a Saudi government mandate to expand exploration beyond the limits set in the original concession agreement.

The concession area granted to Socal by the government in 1933 consisted of an exclusive area covering all of eastern Saudi Arabia, extending to the western reach of the Dahna Sands. In 1939, the concession was extended to include additional areas in the northwest and southwest of the Kingdom. The concession was reduced by subsequent relinquishments until, in 1973, it consisted of six separate pieces covering a total of 84,943 square miles (220,000 sq km).

In 1986, Aramco was reassigned oil exploration rights to all of the territory of the original concession and its supplemental areas. Four years later, the Red Sea coastal strip with adjacent waters was added to the prospective area.

• *Photo: S.M. Amin*

1990 - 1999: Global Reach

1990

Oil production is increased dramatically to stabilize the world market in response to the Gulf crisis.

1991

The company helps combat the Gulf oil spill.

A Saudi Aramco subsidiary buys 35 percent of SsangYong Oil Refining Co. Ltd. (now S-Oil Corporation) in the Republic of Korea.

1992

Oil and gas are discovered on the Red Sea coastal plain.

1993

A Royal Decree consolidates virtually all the Kingdom's refineries, petroleum product distribution facilities, and the government's share in joint ventures, in Saudi Aramco.

1994

Maximum sustained crude oil production capacity is returned to 10 million bpd.

A company subsidiary purchases 40 percent of the shares of Petron Corporation in the Philippines.

Shaybah, 1998 • Photo: H.A. Al-Ramadan

1995

Saudi Aramco CEO and President Ali I. Al-Naimi is named Minister of Petroleum and Mineral Resources.

The program to build 15 advanced supertankers for Vela International Marine Ltd. is completed.

1996

A Saudi Aramco subsidiary purchases 50 percent of Motor Oil (Hellas) Corinth Refineries S.A. and Avinoil Industrial Maritime Oil Company S.A. in Greece.

1997

The company develops POWERS (Parallel Oil-Water-Gas-Reservoir Simulator), a high-resolution reservoir simulator to model and predict the performance of super-giant reservoirs.

1998

A company subsidiary, in partnership with Texaco and Shell, establishes Motiva Enterprises LLC, a major refining and marketing joint venture, superseding Star Enterprise.

Shaybah field comes on-stream.

1999

The Dhahran-Riyadh-Qasim multi-product pipeline and the Ras Tanura Upgrade project are completed.

Geologists, geophysicists and petroleum engineers work together to select drill sites in the company's Exploration and Petroleum Engineering Center (EXPEC) in Dhahran, 1993. EXPEC, inaugurated a decade earlier, is the center for all exploration and petroleum engineering activities, from the laboratory analyses of deep subsurface core samples to the ultimate management of producing oil and gas fields.

1993 also witnessed the ascension of Saudi Arabia to the top spot among oil-producing nations, surpassing the United States and the recently dissolved Soviet Union. • *Photo: A.G. Waine*

Marjan GOSP-2 (gas-oil separation plant) rises from the waters of the Arabian Gulf early in the 1990s. The Marjan project, completed in 1993, was followed closely by projects in the Zuluf field, efforts which substantially raised Arabian Medium crude oil production capacity. The Marjan project included completion of two 250,000 bpd GOSPs and an offshore gas-compression plant with a capacity of 600 million standard cubic feet, one of the largest in the world at the time. • *Photo: A.G. Waine*

On their way to a shirt-sleeves business meeting at Villa Escudero in the Philippines are, left to right, H.E. Fouad al-Faqih, Saudi Arabia's ambassador to the Philippines; Ado Escudero; H.E. Hisham M. Nazer, Saudi Arabian Minister of Petroleum and Mineral Resources; and Ali I. Al-Naimi, president and CEO of Saudi Aramco. Nazer, Al-Naimi and other high-level representatives from the Kingdom and the company were exploring long-term business opportunities in Southeast Asia on their tour of the Philippines, Korea, Japan and China in early 1994.

The early 1990s were times of change, as the company moved from an oil producer to a fully integrated oil and gas company with operations not only in exploration and production, but also in refining, marketing and international shipping. Saudi Aramco developed a truly global reach, forging partnerships in North America, Europe and Asia.
• *Photo: A.Y. Al-Dobais*

The setting sun outlines a drilling rig in the Hawtah region in central Saudi Arabia, south of Riyadh. In 1994, a new grade of crude oil, Arabian Super Light, the highest quality crude ever found in the Kingdom, made its debut, pumped from fields discovered in the central region. The first shipment of Arabian Super Light, from the Yanbu' terminal on the Red Sea, also marked the first Saudi Aramco production from outside the Eastern Province. • *Photo: S.M. Amin / Saudi Aramco World / PADIA*

A masterpiece of nautical engineering, a precisely machined propeller takes shape in the Hyundai shipyard in Korea in 1993. Metal workers shape the propeller with its golden gleam from a solid alloy of bronze, nickel and manganese. • *Photo: A.Y. Al-Dobais*

The *Phoenix Star* receives its final bow section at Mitsubishi's Nagasaki, Japan, shipyard in 1993. Its sister ship and identical twin, the *Al-Bali Star*, shares the dry dock. The pair of supertankers soon joined the *Libra Star*, floated out earlier and undergoing outfitting at the time this photo was taken. • *Photo: A.Y. Al-Dobais*

Like a giant three-dimensional jigsaw puzzle, the *Suhail Star* takes shape in the Odense Lindø A/S shipyard in Denmark in June 1994. The three tankers built here were all classified at more than 300,000 deadweight tons. Vela's specifications for the ships exceeded industry standards and included substantial extra steel, coatings and system controls. • *Photo: A.M. Al-Khalifa*

Vela International Marine Ltd., the shipping subsidiary of Saudi Aramco, was founded in 1984, with four secondhand tankers. In the 1990s, Vela embarked on an ambitious shipbuilding plan to add 15 new Very Large Crude Carriers (VLCCs) to the fleet, each with the capacity to carry more than 2 million barrels of oil. Three tankers were built in Denmark with the others coming from shipyards in either Korea or Japan. The three-year project was completed in March 1995, when the *Alphard Star* was transferred from its Danish builder to Vela. More recently, Vela added four new VLCCs in 2002-2003, bringing the number of owned ships in the fleet to 23 VLCCs and five product tankers, the latter of which ply coastal routes in the Red Sea and Arabian Gulf.

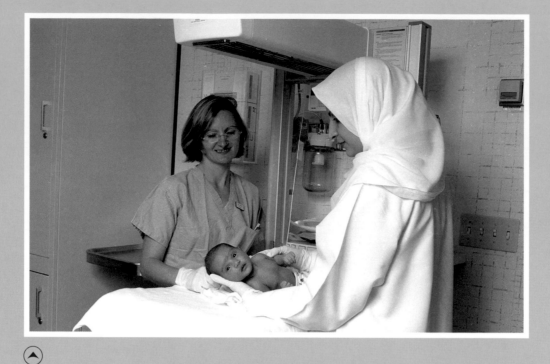

Two Dhahran medical professionals care for an infant on an examination table in March 1999. The previous year, an advanced Oncology Treatment Center opened in Dhahran to provide quality cancer treatment for employees and their dependents. The center provides chemotherapy and radiation treatment to complement existing surgical and chemotherapy modalities. • *Photo: F.I. Al-Dossary*

Future company employees study chemistry in one of the company's training laboratories, 1994. That same year saw the completion of an ambitious expansion program that brought the number of training locations to 10 main facilities and seven satellite locations Kingdomwide, with a total of nearly 730 classrooms and shops. The year before, 7,700 employees were enrolled in training programs.

By 1996, about 80 percent of the nearly 58,000 Saudi Aramco employees were Saudis, and Saudis held 28 of the top 32 offices in the company, compared to 18 of the top 31 top positions in 1984. About 87 percent of the industrial workforce was Saudi, compared to just over 50 percent in 1980. • *Photo: S.M. Amin*

The processing of crude oil takes brawn as well as brains, as can be seen in this photo from Abqaiq in 1994. Nearly 70 percent of all crude produced by Saudi Aramco is stabilized at Abqaiq Plants, the world's largest crude oil processing facility. Saudi crude comes in five grades: Arabian Heavy, Medium, Light, Extra Light and Super Light.
• *Photo: A.G. Waine*

With engine-access panels open and the aircraft undergoing a complete inspection by maintenance personnel, a Boeing 737 receives thorough attention from nose to tail and wingtip to wingtip. The Boeing 737s are part of an aviation fleet that, in 1996, when this photo was taken, included 17 helicopters and 15 fixed-wing aircraft.

Saudi Aramco maintenance crews leave nothing to chance during regular inspections and maintenance of the company fleet. Certified by the FAA and fully trained to perform highly technical procedures, the aircraft maintenance staff applies exacting standards to ensure flight safety and has earned several international safety awards.
• *Photo: A.G. Waine*

The oil spill associated with the 1990-91 Gulf crisis, as seen below from the air in March, was among the world's worst spills and one of the greatest challenges faced — and met — by Saudi Aramco in its history. The company first received word of the spill early on January 25. In addition to the adverse effects on the environment, the oil posed a serious threat to the Kingdom's offshore crude oil production and onshore desalination and power plants that used seawater to produce drinking water and electricity.

The company activated its oil-spill response team and drew upon its own and chartered equipment and supplies to fight the spill.

Crews battled bad weather, an unseasonable shift in winds and the challenges posed by coupling oil-spill fighting equipment from different manufacturers. The force grew to a peak of 450 men, 20 vessels, 40 vacuum tank trucks, 35 skimmer boats and 40 pieces of construction equipment.

Well into April, some 2,000 to 3,000 barrels of oil a day were still spilling into the Gulf from damaged facilities in Kuwait. The flow was finally stopped in early May.

Because of their geographical location, two bays south of Tanajib trapped several hundred thousand barrels of oil, sparing the remainder of Saudi Arabia's east coast considerable additional environmental injury. The company established about a dozen recovery sites around the bays, while large company skimmer ships were assigned to pick up oil in the open Gulf.

Hundreds of Saudi Aramco employees joined the volunteer effort to rescue and clean seabirds, turtles and other animals.

Oil-spill fighting equipment came from Japan, Germany, New Zealand, France, the United Kingdom, Canada, the United States and The Netherlands, including more than 20 miles (32 km) of offshore booms, more than 19 miles (30 km) of oil-absorbent booms and 1.24 miles (2 km) of bay booms, plus at least 16 skimmers.

The company eventually recovered more than 1 million barrels of oil from the Gulf. The spill did not affect the operations of any company or public facility, nor did it damage company industrial facilities or curtail production. In the intervening years, the company has conducted environmental studies and continues to monitor the impacted areas. The coastline has made a remarkable recovery. • *Photo: A.Y. Al-Dobais*

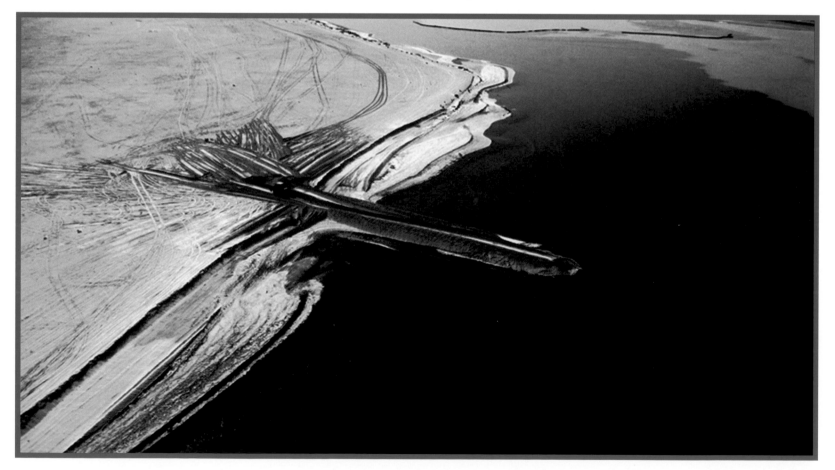

Channels are crisscrossed with booms to deflect oil from coastal installations. • *Photo: R. Johnson / Saudi Aramco World / PADIA*

An oil-soaked bird is recovered for cleaning.
• *Photo: R. Johnson*

Oil-spill teams work long hours installing, repairing and repositioning booms.
• *Photo: R. Johnson / Saudi Aramco World / PADIA*

Dusk falls on the Ras Tanura refinery on the Arabian Gulf north of Dhahran. Ras Tanura is home to both a marine terminal and a refinery. The refinery, seen here, underwent a major upgrade in 1999, the year this photo was taken. Today, the Ras Tanura Refinery, with a capacity of 550,000 barrels per day (bpd), is one of five company refineries with a combined capacity of more than 1 million bpd, the largest refining capacity in the Middle East. • *Photo: A.Y. Al-Dobais*

Shaybah project personnel review a layout of facilities to be constructed as part of the production infrastructure. The project team completed the project proposal packages in February 1996, within seven months from the start of the detailed engineering work. • *Photo: unknown*

Qurian al-Hajri draws a map in the sand for veteran driver Salbokh Khamis. Like Khumayyis ibn Rimthan in the 1930s, in the 1990s, al-Hajri represented a class of company employee who are of Bedouin origin and enjoy an instinctive knowledge of the desert, thus becoming vital for leading truck convoys hundreds of miles across the Rub' al-Khali to the construction site for the Shaybah residential and industrial complex.

During the first quarter of 1996, the company built a road a week on average, using heavy earth-moving equipment to connect the *sabkhahs*, or salt flats, where drilling rigs would operate and facilities would be constructed.
• *Photo: F.I. Al-Dossary*

First discovered in 1968, the Shaybah field was held in inventory until economic conditions and improvements in drilling and other technologies made exploitation of the field feasible.

Located in Saudi Arabia's Rub' al-Khali, or Empty Quarter, 500 miles (800 km) southeast of Dhahran, Shaybah is located in some of the harshest terrain on the globe. Sand dunes tower a thousand feet (333 m) high, winds routinely reach 50 mph (80 kmph), and summer temperatures can soar to 122 degrees Fahrenheit (50 degrees Celsius).

Shaybah holds more than 14 billion barrels of oil — roughly equivalent to the reserves of the North Sea — and some 25 trillion cubic feet of natural gas. Saudi Aramco built a 240-mile (386-km) access road, laid a 401-mile (645-km) pipeline and constructed extensive production, communication, maintenance, support and residential facilities — all in three years, one year earlier than planned. Shaybah came on-stream in 1998.

The 500,000 barrels of Arabian Extra Light crude oil produced in Shaybah each day is equivalent to the daily total energy needs of more than 10 million households.

▶

A new well goes in at Shaybah. More than 140 new oil wells were drilled to produce the field, and such cutting-edge technologies as multi-lateral wells, horizontal drilling and 3D seismic technology were employed to optimize production. • *Photo: H.A. Al-Ramadan*

▲

A bulldozer cuts a swath through the Rub' al-Khali in 1993. Construction of the Shaybah facilities involved moving 30 million cubic meters of sand. • *Photo: S.M. Amin*

Seismic readings are taken from atop a dune at Shaybah, 1993.
• *Photo: S.M. Amin*

The central administration complex at Shaybah includes
accommodation, dining, education and recreation facilities
for 750 personnel. • *Photo: A.Y. Al-Dobais*

▲

Then Crown Prince 'Abd Allah, center, with, on his left, Ali I. Al-Naimi, Minister of Petroleum and Mineral Resources and Chairman of the Board, and, on his right, Abdallah S. Jum'ah, president and CEO, accompanied by members of the royal family and company management — and one young guest — visit the core area complex of Saudi Aramco's Dhahran headquarters. The occasion for the visit was the inauguration of the Dhahran-Riyadh-Qasim multi-product pipeline and the Ras Tanura Refinery upgrade in April 1999. • *Photo: A.Y. Al-Dobais*

◀

A company representative, right, meets with a local manufacturer in Dammam, 1990. Since its earliest days, the company has sought to develop relationships with local manufacturers and service providers. A decade later, Saudi Aramco was placing 88 percent of its purchases with Saudi importers and manufacturers and had launched a contractor website to provide easy access to forms, instructions and other information. Currently, about 12,000 contractors are registered to do business with the company. • *Photo: S.M. Amin*

Nahar, a houbara bustard, accompanied by his friend Jerboa, asks Makar, the desert fox, if he has seen Samarah, Nahar's mate, in this scene from the animated film *Land of Khuzama*. The 26-minute film, in Arabic and English versions, was produced by Saudi Aramco and released in connection with Earth Week 1999. The film, named after a type of local wildflower, delivers an entertaining message about the importance of preserving the environment and underscores the need to respect the Kingdom's wildlife.

The *Land of Khuzama*, and other films such as *Where Does It Come From?* and the award-winning 3-D movie *Energy to the World*, are screened regularly at the Saudi Aramco Exhibit in Dhahran where some 300 students visit each day.

Loading arms frame a supertanker at Ras Tanura, 1990. For the year, a total of 2,350 vessels called at company export terminals at Ras Tanura, Ju'aymah and Yanbu', loading crude oil, refined products and NGL.

In response to the 1990-1991 Gulf crisis, Saudi Aramco significantly boosted crude oil production, from 4.9 million bpd in 1989 to 6.3 million bpd in 1990. By year's end, maximum sustained production capacity had risen to 8.5 million bpd.

The increase in production was made possible by accelerating the timetable and increasing the scope of the Crude Oil Expansion Program, adopted in 1989 to meet long-term market demand. The work, which included recommissioning 146 oil wells, 12 mothballed GOSPs (gas-oil separation plants), and miles of pipelines, as well as associated facilities for gas compression and wet crude handling, marked the greatest challenge to the company and its employees since the huge oil, gas and electrical power projects of the 1970s.
• *Photo: S.M. Amin*

Petron service stations sell gasoline and petroleum products throughout the Philippines. In 1994, Aramco Overseas Company, B.V., a Saudi Aramco subsidiary, acquired a 40-percent stake in Petron Corporation, the Philippines' leading oil refining and marketing company. The refinery in Limay, Bataan, is the largest in the country, with a capacity of 180,000 barrels per day, and Petron products are sold to consumers through a chain of more than 1,100 service stations. Petron also supplies products to local industry.

The agreement gives Saudi Aramco rights to supply much of Petron's total crude oil requirements. In 2004, Petron's market share was 38 percent of the retail market. • *Photo: courtesy Petron*

The S-Oil refinery and harbor complex in Onsan, Korea, seen here in June 1993, is just one part of Saudi Aramco's extensive activities in Southeast Asia. In July 1991, a company affiliate purchased a 35-percent stake in SsanYong Oil, renamed S-Oil in 2000, of Korea.

Today, the Onsan refinery complex has a crude oil refinery with a capacity of 580,000 barrels per day, plus additional refining and petrochemical facilities. S-Oil also operates a chain of branded service stations throughout the country.

The partnership with S-Oil was the first foray into refining and marketing equity and joint ventures in the region. By 2005, Saudi Arabia had become the leading supplier of crude oil to Korea, Japan, China and Taiwan. • *Photo: A.Y. Al-Dobais*

As part of a world-class partnership with Saudi Refining Inc. (SRI), a subsidiary of Aramco Services Company, the Motiva Refinery in Convent, Louisiana, serves a well-established market of some 13,000 service stations throughout a 26-state region along the Atlantic and Gulf Coasts in the United States.

Motiva Enterprises LLC, a major refining and marketing joint venture with Texaco and Shell in the United States, was established in 1998, superseding a previous joint venture established a decade earlier and known as Star Enterprise. Motiva, now an equal partnership between Shell and SRI, is headquartered in Houston, Texas. • *Photo: unknown*

The movement of oil, gas, electric power and refined products is managed on the "big boards" in the Operations Coordination Center (OCC) in Dhahran, the focal point for all supply and distribution operations in the company. The loading and unloading of tankers, the production and distribution of crude oil, gas and refined products and the production of electrical power — all are managed from the OCC.

Twenty-four hours a day, every day of the year, OCC personnel monitor company operations using real-time computer systems connected through an extensive communications network to all of the company's plants, terminals and pipelines. In 2005, the OCC underwent a major renovation in which the displays were replaced by five video walls, using state-of-the-art Digital Light Processing technology. • *Photo: H.A. Al-Ramadan*

2000 - 2005: The New Millennium

2000

The company assumes operation and maintenance of the first of five proposed Saudi Strategic Storage facilities to ensure the supply and distribution of refined products in the event of an emergency.

New logo and corporate identity are launched.

2001

Hawiyah Gas Plant comes on-stream.

The first phase of the Research and Development Center opens in Dhahran.

2002

Texaco's interest in Motiva is acquired. Shell and Saudi Refining Inc., a subsidiary of Aramco Services Co., each own a 50 percent interest of the refining and marketing company operating primarily in the eastern United States.

POWERS, the company's proprietary reservoir simulator, models the entire Ghawar field, the world's largest, in a single 10 million-cell model.

Haradh Gas Plant, 2003 • Photo: K. Childress

2003

Haradh Gas Plant begins operations.

The company signs an agreement with Royal Dutch Shell and TotalFinaElf for upstream gas exploration and production projects in the south Rub' al-Khali.

2004

The Qatif Program comes on-stream.

A company subsidiary acquires a strategic shareholding in Showa Shell, a refining and marketing company in Japan.

Three joint venture agreements for upstream gas projects in the north Rub' al-Khali are made with Lukoil, Sinopec, and a consortium of Eni and Repsol YPF.

2005

Saudi Aramco forms a joint venture with Sumitomo Chemical Co., Ltd. of Japan to develop an integrated refining and petrochemical complex in Rabigh on the Red Sea coast.

A company subsidiary, Sinopec of China and ExxonMobil sign an agreement to expand a refinery in Fujian province, and build downstream petrochemical facilities.

This isn't the crew on the bridge of a spaceship, but company geoscientists and petroleum engineers modeling hydrocarbon reservoirs in a company 3-D Visualization Center in Dhahran, November 2000. The 3-D models are computer-based displays of various integrated sets of data, including seismic data, well logs, core sample analyses, and reservoir simulators. Saudi Aramco's proprietary software, POWERS, (Parallel Oil-Water-Gas-Reservoir Simulator), capable of dynamically modeling large, mature reservoirs at very high spatial resolution and for very long time periods, is also drawn upon.

Several 3-D visualization rooms, which use the latest in integration and projection software, were designed and constructed for Saudi Aramco. These rooms, located in the Exploration and Petroleum Engineering Center (EXPEC), have transformed reservoir modeling into a virtual reality, enabling multi-disciplinary teams of geoscientists and engineers to literally immerse themselves inside the reservoir and probe its secrets. • *Photo: M. Mercer*

Exploration and production work goes on around the clock, ensuring the company meets its commitments to an energy-thirsty world. Advanced technologies play a crucial role in maximizing and sustaining production from the world's largest reserves. Saudi Aramco employs a host of innovative approaches when it comes to drilling, including multi-lateral Maximum Reservoir Contact (MRC) wells to raise recovery rates. The Haradh-III increment will rely exclusively on multi-lateral MRC producing wells.

Another advanced tool is the geosteering of horizontal production wells, in which the drill bit is guided remotely through the targeted layer of the reservoir. In geosteering, real-time drilling, logging and survey data are collected on the drilling site and transmitted to Dhahran and then monitored anywhere in the company via the Intranet. Asset team members, geoscientists and engineers can view and analyze data in EXPEC's 3-D Visualization Center while the drilling continues. • *Photo: M. Mercer*

President and CEO Abdallah S. Jum'ah is joined by Ayidh Al-Farwan, center, a 44-year employee, and Abdel Hameed Al-Ahmadi, a new employee, at the ceremony launching the new logo, April 24, 2000.
• *Photo: A.Y. Al-Dobais*

The logo may have changed, but the spirit remains the same. • *Photo: H.A. Al-Makayyl*

Until 1946, the predecessors of Saudi Aramco, first known as the California Arabian Standard Oil Company (Casoc) and then Aramco (the Arabian American Oil Company) operated under the concessionaire's corporate entity. In June 1946, the company newspaper, then known as the *Sun and Flare*, put out a call for entries to design the first Aramco logo. Employee Harry Flackmeier's design was chosen from 110 responses. The new logo made its debut in 1948 and remained in use for the next 40 years.

After the Saudi Government completed the acquisition of the company's assets and created Saudi Aramco on November 8, 1988, the call went out for a new logo. Company graphic designer 'Abd al-'Aziz al-Radwan came up with the new logo, which entered use in June 1989.

The company received a fresh look as it entered the millennium: a new corporate logo featuring a horizon-spanning burst of energy and environmentally compatible colors of green and blue. The logo is seen on everything, from company aircraft and vehicles to stationery and from community gateways to safety helmets.

The new logo was approved by the Board of Directors in November 1999 and was unveiled in Dhahran on April 24, 2000.

As rare rain clouds clear away, the company's new 737 fleet awaits the start of another business day at the Saudi Aramco terminal in Dammam, January 30, 2003. Flight operations moved to King Fahd International Airport in 2000. Each of the B737-700 aircraft can seat 135 passengers.
• *Photo: H.A. Al-Ramadan*

▲

Storage tanks take shape at the Hawiyah Gas Plant, the first company facility to process non-associated gas (gas not associated with oil production). Hawiyah came on-stream at the end of 2001, four months early and under budget, and can process 1.6 billion standard cubic feet per day (scfd) of raw non-associated gas and can also produce 1.4 billion scfd of sales gas, 170,000 barrels of condensate and 1,000 metric tons of sulfur per day.

The three-year project included three components: gathering (gas wells and manifolds); distribution (expansion of the sales gas grid); and the gas plant and associated facilities. The Master Gas System was extended to the Riyadh area, with sales gas from Hawiyah firing three electric power plants in the Riyadh area, thus freeing 260,000 barrels per day of Arabian Light crude oil for export.
• *Photo: M. Mercer*

▼

Located about 134 miles (220 km) south of Dhahran, the Hawiyah Gas Plant boosted the Kingdom's gas supply by more than 30 percent, fuels electricity grids and water desalination plants, and feeds the country's petrochemical industry.

Roughly 10,000 men of 50 different nationalities worked on the project, the Project Management Institute's Project of the Year for 2002. • *Photo: H.A. Al-Ramadan*

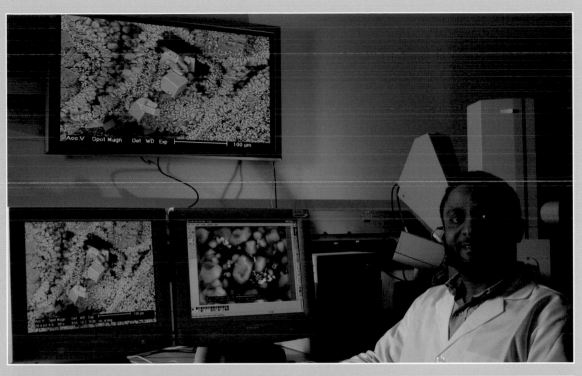

Scanning electron microscope images, seen here on the monitors, are obtained from core samples and studied by geoscientists and lab technicians, such as Abdul Rahman K. Al-Nowaishi, in the Research & Development Center. The images allow researchers to study the porosity and permeability of hydrocarbon reservoirs at the micron level, helping manage the world's most prolific fields.
• *Photo: A.Y. Al-Dobais*

The exterior of the Research & Development Center is a striking sight in the evening.
• *Photo: A.M. Al-Moaiweed*

The lobby of the Research & Development Center.
• *Photo: A.M. Al-Moaiweed*

Company scientists in the Research & Development Center (R&DC) in Dhahran pursue answers to a host of crucial questions: How can petroleum fuels burn cleaner and more efficiently? How can heavy crude oils yield lighter products? What are the best ways to combat corrosion? How can more oil and gas be withdrawn from reservoirs? The R&DC reflects the burgeoning emphasis on research and development and drives the company's far-reaching commitment to meet future demands for energy, create technology-based business ventures, and identify new revenue streams that promote the development of the local economy.

Company scientists at the R&DC have contributed nearly one-third of the company's U.S. patents, some of which have been awarded or are pending for new gasoline-, diesel- and naphtha-based fuel formulations and associated refinery processes.

Housed in a state-of-the-art facility of 33,000 square meters, the Center provides laboratories, pilot plants, workshops, offices and meeting rooms for 330 professional staff members, 75 percent of whom are Saudi nationals. The R&DC is also undertaking joint projects with in-Kingdom and regional research centers, participating in joint industry projects and teaming up with international universities and research centers.

The Haradh Gas Plant, 174 miles (280 km) southwest of Dhahran, is the second Saudi Aramco gas plant to process only non-associated gas (gas produced directly from gas reservoirs and not a secondary product of oil production). Construction began in January 2000, and the plant came on-stream in June 2003, six months ahead of schedule.

Designed to process 1.6 billion standard cubic feet per day (scfd) of a combined raw feed of sweet and sour gas, the plant can deliver 1.5 billion scfd of sales gas to the Master Gas System and 170,000 barrels of condensate to Abqaiq Plants via a 143-mile (230-km) pipeline.

Located at the southern tip of Ghawar, the world's largest onshore oil field, the greater Haradh project includes three Arabian Light crude oil production increments. The first of these increments, Haradh GOSP-1 (gas-oil separation plant), went on-stream in March 1996. The second increment, Haradh GOSP-2, was commissioned in April 2003. The third increment, Haradh GOSP-3, is scheduled to be on-stream in 2006, raising total capacity from Haradh to 900,000 barrels of crude oil per day.
• *Photo: Al-Mohtaraf*

Named Project of the Year for 2004 by the Project Management Institute, Haradh Gas Plant came on-stream at a cost 25 percent under approved funds.
• *Photo: K. Childress*

Ninety-eight percent of the workforce on the Haradh Project development team was composed of Saudi personnel, and in the gas plant itself, 99 percent of the personnel are Saudi.

Projects such as these also have a significant impact on the local economy: For Haradh, local participation in the Gas Program equaled a total of $681 million for engineering in-Kingdom, construction by Saudi contractors and locally manufactured materials. • *Photo: A.Y. Al-Dobais*

An employee tests pipes with a meter gauge at Ras Tanura, 2003. Home to a refinery and a marine terminal, company facilities at Ras Tanura are a major component of Saudi Aramco's operations. Terminal operations began in May 1939, with the loading of the first tanker of Saudi crude aboard the *D.G. Scofield*. Today, the Ras Tanura Terminal can service the largest crude and LPG tankers afloat. Roughly 5 million barrels of oil are loaded on tankers every day at Ras Tanura alone, equivalent to one-fourth of the daily U.S. consumption. • *Photo: Al-Mohtaraf*

⊳ Ameerah A. Al-Mustafa, left, a petroleum engineer with Reservoir Description and Simulation, discusses business with colleague Hashim Hussein. Petroleum engineers concern themselves with the inner architecture of hydrocarbon reservoirs, studying ways to increase their porosity and permeability. Porosity refers to the gaps or pores between grains in the reservoir rock, while permeability is the measure of how well liquids flow through the pores. The average porosity and permeability of Saudi Arabia's reservoirs are among the best in the world.
• *Photo: T.M. Al-Ghamdi*

⊲ Saudi Aramco's fleet of 21 helicopters is kept flying by people such as Mohammed Saeed Al-Hajri, a member of Ground Support at the company's Tanajib facility. Company pilots numbered 64 in 2004. Twenty of the pilots were Saudi nationals, and together, the pilots fly an average of 13,000 hours per year in a variety of missions: Offshore crew changes, Medivac, search and rescue, pipeline and security patrols, and transporting harbor pilots to visiting tankers.
• *Photo: unknown*

⊳ The *Leo Star* is just one of 23 Very Large Crude Carriers (VLCCs) in the fleet of Vela International Marine Ltd., Saudi Aramco's shipping subsidiary. One of four double-hulled VLCCs delivered to Vela in 2002-2003, the *Leo Star*, a 317,000-ton deadweight tanker, was built by Hyundai Heavy Industries in Ulsan, Korea.

Vela (Latin for "sail") is derived from a namesake cluster of stars in the constellation Argo Navis in the Southern Hemisphere. Each ship is named for one of the cluster's stars.

The company celebrated its 20th anniversary in September 2004 and currently ships more than 3 million barrels per day of Saudi crude oil and other products to customers around the globe.
• *Photo: unknown*

Children view one of the displays that vividly demonstrate oil processing technology at the Saudi Aramco Exhibit, 2002. The exterior of the Exhibit can be seen in the top photo. • *Photo: Al-Mohtaraf*

Young girls play in a pool of foam, in a scene from the annual summer family program in 2000 at the Saudi Aramco Exhibit.

Each year, close to 200,000 students, tourists and dignitaries from around the world embark on interactive tours through the Saudi Aramco Exhibit, a facility dedicated to energy education.

Inaugurated in 1987 and upgraded a decade later, the 25,000-square-foot exhibit brings to life Saudi Aramco's work — from exploration, drilling and production, to refining and shipping — while paying tribute to the Arabic and Islamic heritage at its core.
• *Photo: M. Mercer*

It takes a lot of goods — like this sea of pipe — and services to keep Saudi Aramco going, and the company prefers to rely upon Saudi-owned or joint-venture companies when it comes to its contracting, materials, equipment and supply needs.

In 2004, Saudi Aramco executed 1,800 contract actions valued at approximately $5.1 billion, with a preponderance going to Saudi-owned or Saudi joint-venture companies. Purchase orders valued at $1.8 billion were issued to obtain materials, equipment and supplies for oil and gas operations. Of this amount, 89 percent was placed with Saudi manufacturers and vendors, further strengthening local economic growth.
• *Photo: unknown*

Personnel from the Tokyo office of Aramco Overseas Company B.V., and Saudi Petroleum Ltd., Tokyo, share a moment outside their offices in Tokyo. Saudi Aramco is a major supplier of energy to the economies of Asia. In 2004, 46 percent of Saudi Aramco's crude oil exports went to the Far East, as well as 60 percent of its refined products exports and 57 percent of its natural gas liquids (NGL) exports.

Saudi Aramco's original Asian partnerships have flourished, and additional partnerships have followed. In 2004, a company subsidiary acquired a strategic shareholding in Showa Shell Sekiyu K.K. in Japan. The following year, a ceremony in the Fujian province of China broke ground on a project with Sinopec and ExxonMobil to expand a refinery, and build downstream petrochemical facilities.
• *Photo: courtesy SPL Tokyo*

The Qatif Program was the largest crude increment built in the world in the last 25 years. The program included the construction of the Qatif Producing Plants and the expansion and upgrading of both the Berri Gas Plant and the Abu Sa'fah oil field. The Qatif complex came on-stream in July 2004, three months ahead of schedule and within budget.

The Qatif Program also doubled the production of the Abu Sa'fah field and brought on-stream 500,000 bpd of blended Arabian Light crude from the Qatif field, plus 370 million standard cubic feet per day (scfd) of associated gas and 40,000 barrels per day of high-value condensate.

Qatif is the first company facility to produce Arabian Light crude by blending Arabian Extra Light, Arabian Light and Arabian Medium, and it also boasts the largest cogeneration plant in the company.

▲

The Saudi Aramco team that supervised the development, construction and commissioning of all the Qatif facilities was nearly 100 percent Saudi. The plants are currently operated by 100 percent Saudi staff. Overall, more than 86 percent of the total Saudi Aramco work force is Saudi. • *Photo: H.A. Al-Makayyl*

▲

One of the columns of the Qatif Central Producing Facilities glows against the evening sky. All the structural steel — some 13,000 tons — used in the construction of the plants, and all the vessels, were made in-Kingdom. • *Photo: A.Y. Al-Dobais*

Company volunteers and local children come together to plant mangrove seedlings on the Arabian Gulf. Long before corporate social responsibility entered the vocabulary of business, Saudi Aramco was engaged in community development. In the early years, these programs focused on basic health and education. With the growth of governmental agencies and public sector programs, the company shifted its emphasis to providing social assistance activities.

The company regularly sponsors volunteer clean-up campaigns of local desert areas and beaches and reaches thousands of other children through its Children's Art Contest, its fleet of Mobile Libraries and visits to the Saudi Aramco Exhibit. Working with local schools, thousands of mangrove seedlings have been planted along the shores of the Gulf. For the 'Id al-Fitr, the holiday marking the end of Ramadan, the company conducts a Gifts for Orphans campaign. And, on 'Id al-Adha, the holiday marking the end of the hajj, company volunteers stage special events for the handicapped and elderly members of local communities. • *Photo: M.A. Al-Hashem*

⊙

The place could be Hawiyah or Haradh, Qatif, Rabigh, Khursaniyah or any number of Saudi Aramco projects or joint ventures, big and small, anywhere the company operates, but the people are the same: Saudi Aramco people. For nearly eight decades, the people of Saudi Aramco, drawn from across the globe, have met the world's energy needs. • *Photo: K. Childress*

⊙

The Dhahran core area at twilight, October 16, 2000, as seen from Jabal Dhahran, near the site of the first commercial oil discovery in March 1938. The transformation of Dhahran, from geologists' camp to wildcat drilling site to global headquarters of the world's largest and most reliable supplier of energy has driven the development of the Kingdom itself and helped make possible the high standard of living enjoyed by the United States, Europe and Asia. • *Photo: M. Mercer*

Company CEOs

Harry D. Collier
1944 - 1951

William S.S. Rodgers
1951 - 1952

Fred A. Davies
1952 - 1959

Norman Hardy
1959 - 1961

Thomas C. Barger
1961 - 1969

Robert I. Brougham
1969 - 1970

Company Presidents

F.A. Davies	**W.F. Moore**	**R.L. Keyes**	**N. Hardy**	**T.C. Barger**	**R.I. Brougham**
1940 - 1947	1947 - 1952	1952 - 1957	1958 - 1959	1959 - 1968	1968 - 1969

Chairmen of the Board of Directors

R.C. Stoner	**H.D. Collier**	**W.S.S. Rodgers**	**F.A. Davies**	**N. Hardy**	**T.C. Barger**
1943 - 1944	1944 - 1951	1951 - 1952	1952 - 1959	1959 - 1968	1968 - 1969

On May 29, 1933, the oil concession agreement was signed between Saudi Arabia and Standard Oil Company of California (Socal).
On November 8, 1933, a subsidiary, California Arabian Standard Oil Company (Casoc), was created to manage the concession.

Liston F. Hills
1971 - 1973

Frank Jungers
1973 - 1977

John J. Kelberer
1978 - 1988

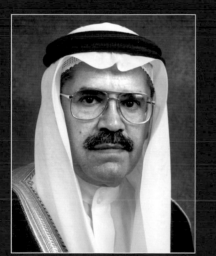

Ali I. Al-Naimi
1988 - 1995

Abdallah S. Jum'ah
1995 -

| **L.F. Hills** | **F. Jungers** | **R.W. Powers** | **H.H. Goerner** | **A.I. Al-Naimi** | **A.S. Jum'ah** |
| 1969 - 1971 | 1971 - 1973 | 1973 - 1978 | 1978 - 1983 | 1984 - 1995 | 1995 - |

| **R.I. Brougham** | **L.F. Hills** | **F. Jungers** | **J.J. Kelberer** | **H.M. Nazer** | **A.I. Al-Naimi** |
| 1969 - 1970 | 1970 - 1973 | 1973 - 1978 | 1978 - 1988 | 1988 - 1995 | 1995 - |

Casoc operated until January 1944, when the company's name changed to the Arabian American Oil Company (Aramco). On November 8, 1988, the Saudi Arabian Oil Company (Saudi Aramco) was established. The photographs in this gallery date from the formation of Aramco.

Saudi Aramco Operations

Saudi Aramco has grown from essentially an exploration and production company, prior to the 1990s, to what it is today: an integrated global petroleum enterprise. The company not only markets and exports crude oil, petroleum products, natural gas liquids and sulfur — it also ships crude oil worldwide through an affiliated company and participates in joint ventures and affiliates at home and abroad to refine crude oil and market its products.

Since 1998, company subsidiaries have formed partnerships with major refiners and marketers in the United States, China, the Republic of Korea, Japan and the Philippines. (A Saudi Aramco subsidiary divested its ownership interest in Motor Oil (Hellas) Corinth Refineries S.A. and Avinoil Industrial Maritime Oil Company S.A. in Greece in late 2005.) In support of international activities, direct and indirect subsidiary offices are located in the United States, the United Kingdom, the Netherlands, Singapore, Japan and China.

Saudi Aramco facilities include refineries located on both coasts of Saudi Arabia and in the capital, Riyadh. The company's major crude oil and NGL export terminals are at Ras Tanura and Ju'aymah on the Gulf and at Yanbu' on the Red Sea.

Affiliates & Principal Export Routes

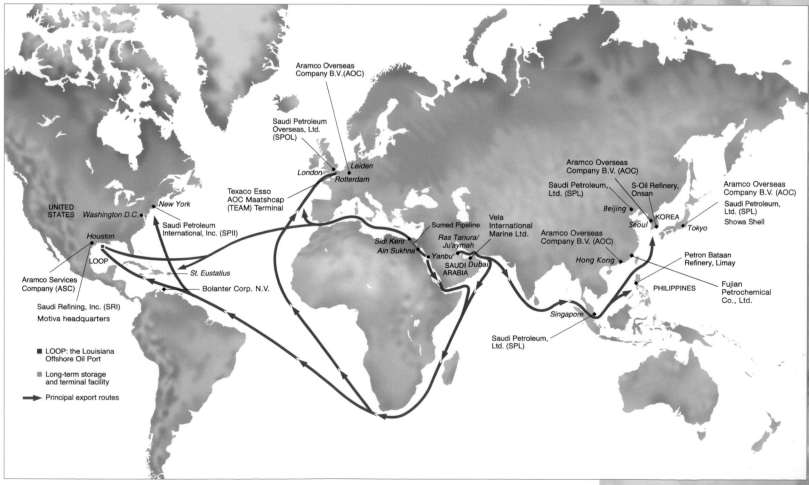

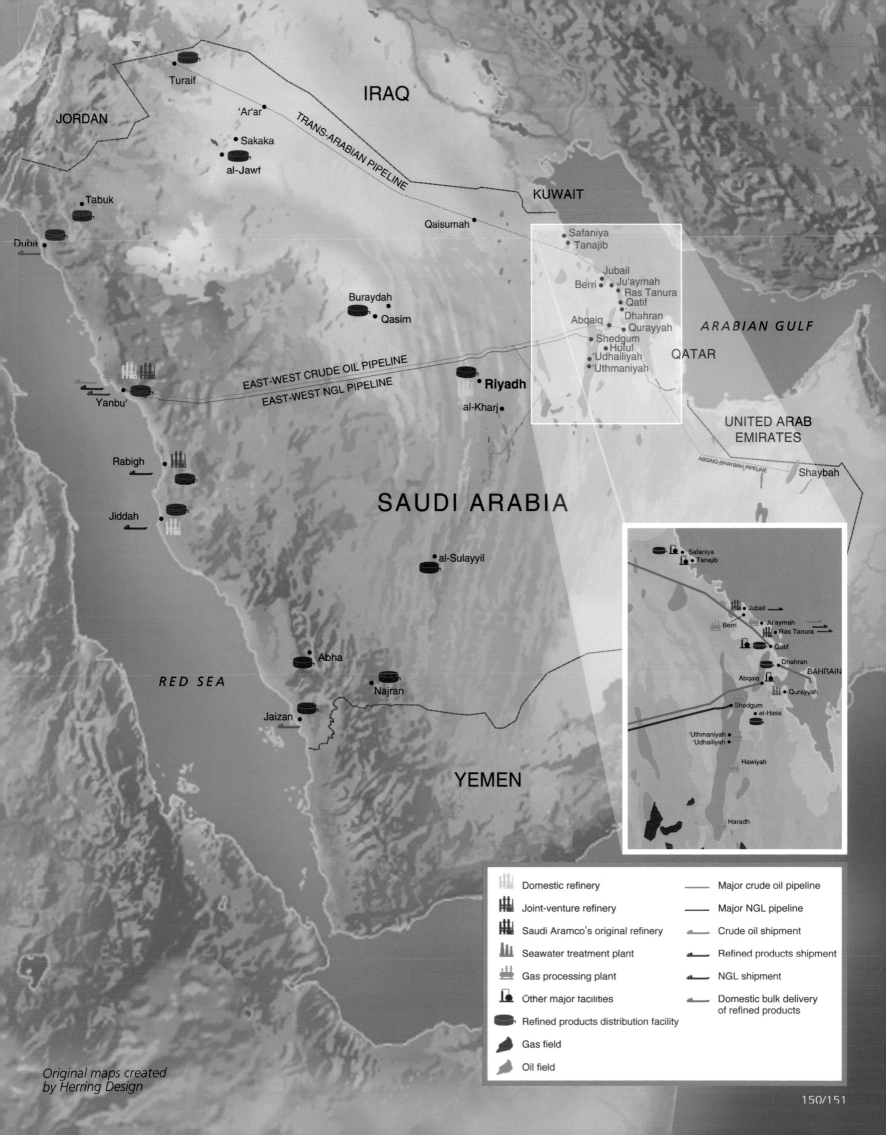

IRAQ

JORDAN

Turaif

'Ar'ar

Sakaka

al-Jawf

Tabuk

KUWAIT

Duba

Qaisumah

TRANS-ARABIAN PIPELINE

Safaniya

Tanajib

Jubail

Ju'aymah

Berri

Ras Tanura

Qatif

Dhahran

Abqaiq

Qurayyah

ARABIAN GULF

Shedgum

Hofuf

'Udhailiyah

QATAR

'Uthmaniyah

Buraydah

Qasim

EAST-WEST CRUDE OIL PIPELINE

EAST-WEST NGL PIPELINE

Yanbu'

Riyadh

al-Kharj

UNITED ARAB
EMIRATES

ABQAIQ-SHAYBAH PIPELINE

Shaybah

Rabigh

Jiddah

SAUDI ARABIA

al-Sulayyil

RED SEA

Abha

Najran

Jaizan

YEMEN

Safaniya

Tanajib

Jubail

Berri

Ju'aymah

Ras Tanura

Qatif

Dhahran

BAHRAIN

Abqaiq

Qurayyah

Shedgum

al-Hasa

'Uthmaniyah

'Udhailiyah

Hawiyah

Haradh

Domestic refinery	Major crude oil pipeline	
Joint-venture refinery	Major NGL pipeline	
Saudi Aramco's original refinery	Crude oil shipment	
Seawater treatment plant	Refined products shipment	
Gas processing plant	NGL shipment	
Other major facilities	Domestic bulk delivery of refined products	
Refined products distribution facility		
Gas field		
Oil field		

*Original maps created
by Herring Design*

Company Photographers

Just as important as the people in front of the camera are the photographers behind it. This book would not be possible had the company not realized early on that it should document the efforts of its people for posterity. This foresight, as well as the artistry and dedication of company photographers (both professional and amateur) allows us to share a split-second in time with some of the people who have made Saudi Aramco, and, in part, Saudi Arabia and the world, what they are today.

The rich photographic archives of Saudi Aramco can be explored online, through a pair of websites.

The first is Saudi Aramco's online archive, accessible via the company's website at *www.saudiaramco.com*. Visitors should select Media Gallery to choose from hundreds of photographs organized into seven categories, including Historical, Downstream, Technology, Health/Educational and others. Photos in low, medium and high resolution can be downloaded through a simple registration process.

Visitors to the website can also view company videos, and read annual reports, speeches and news stories. Company publications are also available on the website, including *Saudi Aramco World*, *Saudi Aramco Journal of Technology*, and *Dimensions*. *The Energy Within* is also available on the website in PDF format.

The other archive is known as PADIA, the Public Affairs Digital Image Archive, built and maintained by Aramco Services Company in Houston, Texas. This is one of the world's largest online photographic archives specializing in contemporary images of the Middle East and the Islamic World.

Most of the more than 25,000 images are published and unpublished photographs from *Aramco World*, 1964-2000, and its successor, *Saudi Aramco World*, to the present. The site includes a slide show highlighting the magazine's first half-century and a search feature.

The archive is accessible via the award-winning *Saudi Aramco World* website, *www.saudiaramcoworld.com*.

In early June 1934, late in the first season in the field, Hugh Burchfiel and R.C. "Dick" Kerr use the Fairchild aerial camera to take panoramic photographs to complete the detailing of the Dammam Dome. • *Photo: J.W. Hoover / Saudi Aramco World / PADIA*

Joe Mountain washes film in this undated photograph. While the Fairchild 71 aircraft was being modified in Maryland, R.C. "Dick" Kerr spent two weeks in Rochester, New York, home of the Eastman Kodak company. There, he and Kodak researchers developed special methods for processing photographic film in the harsh desert conditions. • *Photo: R.C. Kerr*

Sheikh Amin joined Aramco in 1948, studied photography in his off time and joined the Photo Unit in 1965, eventually rising to the position of chief photographer. Amin retired in 1985, but continued to take photos for the company as a contractor. • *Photo: unknown*

Dorothy Miller served four stints with Aramco, the first in 1947 and the last from 1967 to 1977. An avid photographer, her 14 volumes of photographs of the Kingdom and the company are part of Saudi Aramco's extensive archives. Miller is seen here in 1950 with Sinafi, one of the Bedouin "relators" who shared their linguistic and geographical knowledge with the company's Arabian Research Division of Government Relations. • *Photo: D. Miller*

Aramco's chief photographer, Burnett H. Moody (kneeling, front) and his Photo Unit staff, left to right: V.K. Antony, Sa'id Al-Ghamdi, Ali Mohammed Khalifa, Ali Abdulla Khalifa, Ahmed Mentakh and Abdul Latif Yousif, gather around Well No. 7, the discovery well, in Dhahran in 1962. • *Photo: C.E.W.*

Saudi Aramco's chief photographer, Abdullah Y. Al-Dobais (kneeling, in reddish shirt) and the Photo Unit staff, left to right: Hussain A. Al-Ramadan, Abdulaziz M. Al-Moaiwced, Tariq M. Shuja (supervisor, Photo Lab), Faisal I. Al-Dossary, Hassan M. Al-Turaiki, Hadi A. Al-Makayyl, and Turki M. Al-Ghamdi, gather around Well No. 7 in Dhahran, February 6, 2005. • *Photo: J. Timbang / Abu Abdul Aziz Studio*